FAITH

in the age of uncertainty

You can do very little with faith,
But you can do nothing without it.

– Samuel Butler

Words cannot reveal him. Mind cannot reach him. Eyes do not see him. How then can he be comprehended, save when taught by those seers who indeed have known him?

– Katha Upanishad

FOREWORD

In his poem "Dover Beach," Matthew Arnold has a famous verse on Faith:

> The Sea of Faith
> Was once, too, at the full, and round earth's shore
> Lay like the folds of a bright girdle furled.
> But now I only hear
> Its melancholy, long, withdrawing roar,
> Retreating, to the breath
> Of the night-wind, down the vast edges drear
> And naked shingles of the world.

Although written in the nineteenth century, the words have a strange resonance as we enter the twenty-first, and the whole question of Faith presents itself before us in a new perspective.

Although Faith is not necessarily tied to any particular religious dogma, it is often looked upon as a fundamental aspect of religious belief. Thus followers of various religions have "Faith" in their own religious traditions and in the divinity as their religion sees it. There can also be secular faiths – such as faith in communism, in democracy, in progress, in science, and so on. Nonetheless, what we are really dealing with is what Hermes Trismegistus calls the "Fair Faith," which means faith in something that is deeper, higher and nobler than our mundane consciousness, what Shelley calls "the devotion to something afar from the sphere of our sorrow." The word Faith also resonates with the Sanskrit word *Shraddha*, which plays such a significant role in Hindu theology.

The whole question of faith has assumed renewed significance in the light of the traumatic events that have taken place in the very first year of the third millenium AD. Where do we draw the line between faith and fanaticism. How do we avert a clash of civilizations based essentially upon religious foundations as postulated by Huntingdon? How does India withstand the crisis that has been released as a result of the shocking events of 11th September and the war in Afghanistan that followed inexorably and is still raging? These are questions which need deep thought and analysis.

The IIC Quarterly in its special issues deals with many areas of current concern and interest. Sima Sharma, in a special issue of the IIC Quarterly on Faith, presented an array of articles by a fascinating spectrum of creative thinkers in India and abroad. This has now been brought out in the form of a book, which will not only be a source of inspiration but will also promote some soul-searching and creative introspection as we hurtle into the future, astride the irreversible arrow of time.

Tarankingh

CONTENTS

Sima Sharma

Introduction

Believer, non-believer or iconoclast, no one living in this *kaliyuga* can be indifferent to this issue. This anthology on the theme of Faith is an offering that comes with a plea that it be read slowly, a little at a time, for it is not "ten easy steps to a better millennium." In fact it has no agenda whatever on the faith question, except to clear a space wide enough for various shades of insights which we might receive and reflect upon. Necessarily, not all thoughts are familiar to everybody, nor have they been homogenized for instant consumption. Yet they do touch our life as it is lived today.

Where does one look for faith – but right here? Down a side of the congested street, joining hospitals at one end and the serenity of Sri Aurobindo Ashram at the other, a leper-cart makes its way; the man pushes it with the woman crouching on the low seat; both wear bandages on hands and feet. He bends down to say something and she looks up – eyes light up and twinkle. The traffic flows on bumper to bumper. Two school children, a girl holding a little boy by the hand, step off the curb to cross. My three-wheeler brakes to an angular stop and so do the other vehicles, turn by turn. Through the chaos the children hop, skip and run across. The Red Sea had heaved for Moses to cross with his people. The gap appeared and closed.

The plane flies over the English Channel – over Dunkirk? Dover? It is a murky day at Heathrow. The young woman in uniform is smart, sharp and competent. Has she a small child at home – perhaps an aged mother? The cab runs smoothly, curving past roundabouts on the immaculate road, past warehouses, past some tidy patches of green. "It's not so good here, mum," says the cabbie. His family back home in Ghana, he feels, are better off and "maybe I'll go home after I've saved some." The ride is over and he's gone. Where is "home"? My best friend lost her husband some months ago. She breaks down as we embrace. "I feel he has just gone down the road for a walk, and I'm waiting to put the tea on." I miss their dog with the soulful eyes. It died a year ago. There used to be an apple tree in the next garden. It has gone too. Two little girls play in that space.

Ordinary lives, ordinary struggles, carrying on with something like extraordinary fortitude. Not waiting for anything, not looking for miracles. Just following the road and doing the next thing to do. "What do you want me to write?" asks the famous scholar. She wrote the history of God and has lived through the twists and turns of an extraordinary life. What can I say? The friend who had introduced us has gone to live in Bosnia, leaving behind stacks of poetry collected over the years in a flat in Belgravia. In Sarajevo there are roadside cafes, they say, and life bubbles over in the evenings. Sarajevo lives on – the TV blares on about Kossovo. Faces flicker on and off the screen. It was the same when it was Iraq, Rwanda, Ethiopia and cyclone-hit settlements. People, carrying bundles and children, trudging on to somewhere else. Then the next slot.

Where does one look for faith but here? Through all the big and small things of life, what does one look for but faith? Between London and Delhi, it flows through the inner city's dreary lanes and the narrow *gallis* lined with warrens of homes behind tacky shops in the front street. Or through stately boulevards. The mix is the same.

However, faith is generally seen as belonging to the exalted area of religion or to religious beliefs and as something opposed to reason. Some have it, they say, and others do not. This is of course open to question and has been explored by those writers in this volume who have chosen to focus either on their own inner journey or on the human being's relationship with the universe. Some make a sharp distinction between faith and belief, others do not. Their one common ground is our sense of awe and wonder.

Religion, with faith as its premise, has of course played a major role in the events of historical and contemporary times. It has provided the basis and the principles for ethics and moral philosophy. This was contested by the rise of scientific humanism in the West and by radical movements all over the world in the secular twentieth century. These issues too have been addressed here: war and justice, wealth and poverty, human rights and individualism as also the spread of social disintegration. The record of religion in undermining faith and human well-being stands alongside its positive contribution. Justifying the unjustifiable in order to promote power interests, religion has come to lose credibility and fallen into fanaticism at the same time. But faith is a live issue, even more so now as it breaks out of its traditional territory – the creeds of our ancestry.

The calendar has marked the passing of a terrible and turbulent century. Our horizons have widened, the world has shrunk and information exploded. The shape of our lives has changed beyond recognition in the space of two generations, and "cultures" are being stowed away in museums. The more things change, however, the more earnestly we delve to find our roots. Beneath the hectic discourse on cultures and identities there lies a simple question, that of human dignity and self-worth.

Although such terms can be intellectually understood and accepted entirely within the framework of rationalism, somehow they do not come to life nor operate at the level of behavior. All the laws and resolutions in the world have brought us not a jot nearer to a reasonable order. The impulse is missing. It eludes the rationalist's structures for it lives in the depth of intent, not upon the plane of knowledge. A mindset which can produce such an impulse – could we call that "faith"? Could it be a way of knowing and doing which makes us what we are, working more in mystery than in organized order?

Mystery was banished from the legitimate areas of knowledge and experience. Tremendous gains were made thereafter which no one can deny. And yet we delve for our roots still, among the fragments of our collective human memory. The simplistic rejection of an entire dimension of life was neither reasonable nor perhaps necessary for the sake of progress. Innocence, once lost, cannot return but the will to live does demand the numinous certitudes that sustained life from the beginning, and today, demands it from a faith more conscious and sophisticated than of old. Without that we may not live, literally.

Many of us feel that a new and affirmative sense of the Sacred is necessary and may even be possible, given a mature and receptive consciousness. It will need to arise from the totality of our knowledge and experience not excluding any part of it – spiritual or material. Technology too is as much an integral part of our experience as is music, art or worship, but we cannot afford to deify it as magic once was.

The questions looming over our times are: what will it mean to be human in the new age? Will humanity benefit from some of the insights offered by our several faith traditions and by the pool of our common universal heritage? Will human consciousness need to alter in a radical manner? These questions may be as old as time, but each age and culture raises them from its own particular ground and context. So far, from age to age, there has been faith that the answers will be found.

The work on this volume has tried to set aside the old fences – between belief and disbelief, between different religions and those that define spaces for philosophy, art or science. This opening process itself has brought about a powerful statement: Faith, like freedom, belongs to no one, but is *that* to which all things belong. In the cosmic order as well as in individual lives, it is that which propels each being towards its own fulfilment, always pushing the goal a little further.

It is not easy to work with the English noun "faith" for it bristles with its own local problems, changing meaning with every use, even as from singular to plural. More complex are the problems we encounter when we begin to speak from our own locations within different cultures and world-views – not one of them exempt today from the preponderance of terms, modes and values of Euro-American culture.

The European experience has revolved around the great clash between religion and reason and the subsequent long debate on science versus God which whittled Divinity down to the "blind watchmaker." Even though Galileo and Copernicus had lost the earlier battle, it did seem as if Newtonians and Darwinians had won the day. But science and reason did not quite win the war. The arrival of Einstein, and what followed, seemed to suggest that it might have been a phony war after all. Ultimately, neither side won. On the one hand, churches have been emptying across the West, but on the other, new creeds and cults are sprouting and large fortunes are being made by the spiritual self-help business. It would be no exaggeration to say that the West is still waiting for God.

However, the experience of the rest of humanity in the non-western world has not been similar. Speaking from India, one could never quite comprehend the rigid distinction between faith and reason or between imagination and thought. The terms *jnana* and *vijnana*, standing for spiritual wisdom and science, were never frozen to mutual exclusion, but were understood as merely two ways in which consciousness reflects the universe, and it was intellectually acceptable that the two may flow into confluence as we approach creative discovery. Faith is known as *shraddha*, a sense of reverence in which the being is poised to participate in the cosmic work – be it through intellectual, artistic, moral or mundane utilitarian activity. It is that which moves one to craft a statue, compose a hymn, rule a kingdom, or sow the seed on the land. It is also that which drives a Buddha or a Ramana Maharishi on their quest. Reverence comes when all that one does belongs to the whole, the All – and that alone is sacred.

Not being bound by the numerical compulsion of monotheism nor by an anthropocentric view of the universe, here in India, it was possible to talk of Divinity, transcending various man-made barriers. The trouble with faith, however, is that it has to be lived as well, both in spirit and in the material world. It remains only talk, or at best very private, if automobiles choke land and air, if rivers die and the holy mountains are stripped of green. Faith cannot be rammed down our throats and it wilts if the Me-generation loses the sense of its impersonal, universal and sacred dimension. It crumbles when defenders of faith execute their missions literally, for faith is the subtle essence that holds and protects our actions, not otherwise.

East or West, we have arrived at the same point – empty church matched by empty ritual, commodification of the spiritual by the lumpenization of it, from desacralization of the mind to desecration of lands. From the Pacific coast to Africa and the South, right round the planet again, the old world is convulsed over the same issue of faith. No less than the West, the rest is also vitally engaged. And pain is shared in real time. Yet, precisely because we feel the pain, we know that we live. And we have hope. Humanity, pushed to the brink has not given up, nor has faith abandoned us yet.

This collection of papers is but a tribute to the spirit that lives in humanity. The volume has no pretensions of representing any cross-section of opinion nor even that of working towards a coherent set of answers. It came into being through the unique authenticity and generosity of each of the contributors. Beyond this articulate circle are people, far too many to count, who were moved by the same impulse to make the idea happen. But there *is* a place which needs to be named where the spirit lingers: the India International Centre, Delhi, where the idea began, toiled and took shape. To all these people, and to the All, my Namaskar.

At first was neither Being nor Nonbeing.
There was not air nor yet sky beyond.
What was its wrapping? Where? In whose
    protection?
Was Water there, unfathomable and deep?

There was no death then, nor yet
    deathlessness;
of night or day there was not any sign.
The One breathed without breath, by its
    own impulse.
Other than that was nothing else at all.

That out of which creation has arisen,
whether it held it firm or it did not,
He who surveys it in the highest heaven,
He surely knows or maybe He does not!

Rig Veda

Kathleen Raine

THE GROUND OF FAITH

F aith is one of the three "theological virtues" of the Christian
religion, together with Hope and Charity (love) and is described
by St. Paul as "the substance of things hoped for, the evidence
of things not seen." The passage continues, "Through faith we
understand that worlds were formed by the word of God, so
that things which are seen were not made of things which do
appear" (Hebrews 11.1-3). The reigning Sovereign of England
bears the title *fidei defensor* (defender of the faith). *The* faith, within
Christendom, is understood to be the Christian religion as such,
and in England to be Church of England "as by law established,"
but our Prince of Wales in a broadcast speech to the nation
expressed his intention to be the "defender of *faith*," which includes,
in modern England, not only Jews and Catholics but also Hindus,
Buddhists, Sikhs and Jains, Muslims and all world religions. Of
course, the belief that the world of appearances is formed by
invisible causes is common to all spiritual traditions, including the
Hellenistic philosophy.

The opposite of faith is doubt, which is so prevalent in the
modern West and westernized world as to have become itself a
kind of orthodoxy, claiming the authority of science, culminating

in the latest theory that the universe was created not by the "word of God" but by a "big bang," purposeless and meaningless. Thus "faith" has become radically undermined, and is no longer regarded as a virtue rather the reverse, since the ground of "faith" has simply disappeared from modern cosmology. The reversal of values this implies may well be the cause of the psychological breakdown of whole societies, who have lost that sense of security which is essential to life itself. In this respect "faith" is innate.

We open our eyes at birth on a world whose reality and security we do not doubt – the love of our nurturing mother, shared with the whole animal kingdom, the certainty of day and night, earth and sky, the whole phenomenal world is firmly established and we ourselves in it. In this sense faith is a norm, proper to our nature as human beings adapted to our given world. The *sanatana dharma*, the "perennial philosophy," relates us to our reality and adapts us to our environment in the most immediate sense, and also in the larger sense as our knowledge grows.

The Vedic hymns, civilization's heritage from time immemorial, express the dawning of faith in this sense, as mankind experienced the emergence of living agents, the "gods," of both inner and outer worlds, still inseparably one: Usha, goddess of dawn and of promise, Savitr the rising sun and awakening consciousness, beginning and setting forth, Surya the sun in his glory and the fullness of life. The world is experienced as an eternal epiphany, as it is in St. Paul's words, formed not by "things which do appear" but "by the word of God."

Loss of this so-to-say innate biological faith in the phenomenal worlds is a psychological malady, a sort of insanity. This indeed I experienced for myself when at the age of twelve or thirteen, shaken by the sudden death of a cousin, the surrounding world became unreal to me and I walked in a *nihil* from which I found relief only by holding my father's hand. This can, I think, be described as a "loss of faith" of an extreme kind: nothing was itself, things were visible and tangible but not present in any other sense. Blake, England's one prophetic poet, described this state when he wrote:

If the sun and moon should doubt
They'd immediately go out.

Mine was a passing psychological crisis, but Blake in these words was challenging the mentality of doubt which was already invading England and France at the end of the eighteenth century. In the wake of the French Revolution it was already becoming current to:

Charge visionaries with deceiving
And call men wise for not believing.

Blake writes of "the Void outside Existence" and he was referring to the rationalist materialist atheism already current at that time, and he names Voltaire and Rousseau as mockers of faith:

Mock on, mock on, Voltaire, Rousseau,
Mock on, mock on, 'tis all in vain,
You throw the sand against the wind
And the wind throws it back again.
And every sand becomes a Gem
Reflected in the beams divine,
Blown back, they blind the mocking eye
But still in Israel's tents they shine.

Blake's lonely prophetic voice denounced the encroaching loss of faith in the name of the Imagination, which Blake saw as the divine presence in man, the "divine humanity" which he identifies with the universal Christ, "Jesus, the Imagination." In his poem "Milton" (type of the "inspired man") the poet whose "Savior" is "the Divine Humanity," the Imagination, declares that he comes "in the grandeur of Inspiration":

To cast off rational demonstration by faith in the Savior and
To cast off Bacon and Locke and Newton from Albion's covering
To take off his filthy garments and clothe him with Imagination and
To cast aside from Poetry all that is not Inspiration
That it shall no longer dare to mock with the aspersion of Madness

Cast on the Inspired....
To cast off the idiot Questioner who is always questioning
But is never capable of answering ...
Who publishes doubt and calls it knowledge, whose Science is
    Despair,
Whose pretence to knowledge is envy, whose whole
    Science is
To destroy the wisdom of ages to gratify ravenous Envy.

Blake's eloquent words are also exact, and during the nineteenth century the claim of doubt to be knowledge made great headway and the attitude voiced by Tennyson in the words "There is more faith in honest doubt than half the creeds" was widespread.

But "faith" is not a matter of credulity or credence. The Apostle's Creed, central to both Catholic and Anglican weekly services, and repeated by the whole congregation, begins with the words "I Believe ..." and is followed by a string of affirmations of belief to which every Christian is asked to subscribe. But "belief" is not "faith": belief is rational and voluntary, or may be mere opinion, whereas faith is a living experience, which turns sand-grains into gems, and by which the earth becomes "full of gods" and (to quote Blake again) the sun is no longer "a round disk, somewhat like a guinea" but "an Innumerable company of the Heavenly host crying Holy, Holy, Holy is the Lord God Almighty." Blake's vision is that of the Vedic hymns. The phenomena are created and preserved by the "word of God" which, both for Blake and for the mainstream Indian tradition, is the divine presence in man, called by Blake the "divine humanity" or (Jesus being God made Man in the Christian creed) "Jesus the Imagination," an understanding that comes close to the Upanishadic understanding of the Self. Faith is an imaginative experience, not a formulated "belief."

Of this experience not factual information but the arts are the normal expression. India, the supreme civilization of the arts of the Imagination, has from time immemorial flowered not only in the arts of poetry, painting, music, sculpture and architecture but also in the grassroots culture of making pottery and textiles, household everyday things – lamps, mirrors, boxes, nut-crackers, musical instruments, things of imaginative beauty and delight. In the words of Jesus, "Man does not live by bread alone but by every word of God." Materialist societies both communist and capitalist have disregarded these words and created social systems providing whole populations with "bread alone," and in the capitalist West material goods in excess, but without beauty and without imaginative food for the soul. No amount of psychological "therapy" can make up for the lost vision.

I had the honor to know India's great daughter, the late Kamaladevi Chattopadhyay, who accomplished the miracle of restoring thousands of displaced people entering India from Pakistan at the time of Partition, from despair to hope. She restored their sense of dignity by founding a co-operative community which was self-sufficient in producing its own food and means of livelihood, but at the same time she understood that the soul too must be fed, and she encouraged theatre and music and above all, the arts and crafts produced by human hands. The marvellous skills of the innate creativity of India's simplest people: beauty and delight, she understood, are not a luxury but a necessity and that surely has been the secret of India's civilization, in which pottery, textiles, metal-work and carved wood, carpets and beads and bracelets are of priceless value not only because they are things of beauty but because they give those who make them the fulfillment of giving expression to their imaginative creativity. Machines can never satisfy the need not only to admire beautiful objects but to create them; Blake called poetry, music and painting "the three Powers in man of conversing with Paradise." Might we not say that "Paradise" is the object of "faith" and is both created and experienced by the Imagination?

Why was it that "doubt" gained ground, credence, and respectability throughout the nineteenth century, and "loss of faith" became a vogue among the educated classes? The Protestant Reformation called in question many things that had passed as certitudes, and Western Christianity had no tradition of spiritual practise such as has always been central in the Orient; Christianity has always been an exoteric not an esoteric religion, whence its reliance on creeds rather than experience. Was it because the

Industrial Revolution deprived whole populations of the simple satisfactions of making and doing creative handiwork? That *sanatana dharma* which Blake calls "the wisdom of ages" has been progressively undermined by Western education, and especially by scientific "research." The world of science is an ever-changing world, innately unstable, always holding out promises but at the same time undermining certainties. In modern universities students are encouraged to "think for themselves"; teaching has moved from the older norm of imparting and transmitting knowledge to the Socratic method of evoking knowledge from the student. Well and good for Socrates demonstrating by questioning an ignorant boy in order to demonstrate that mathematical knowledge is innate and needs only to be evoked, but not so good when F. R. Leavis in Cambridge trained students to call in question the images of Shelley's "Ode to the West Wind" rather than experiencing them as imaginative symbols.

Yeats gave a simple answer when near the end of his life he wrote in a letter: "It seems to me that I have found what I wanted. When I seek to put all in a phrase I say 'Man can embody truth but he cannot know it.' I must embody it in the completion of my life. The abstract is not life and everywhere draws out its contradictions. You can refute Hegel but not the Saint or the Song of Sixpence...." Yeats, it should be remembered, is Blake's first editor and greatest disciple and he too proclaims the supremacy of the Imagination. It is not surprising that Yeats proceeded from his early studies of Blake to his final commitment to the teachings of the *Upanishads*, of ten of which he made, with his teacher Shree Purohit Swami, a most beautiful translation. Yeats's words seem to me a statement of "faith" in its true sense, as obedience to a reality beyond human reason, better described as "revelation."

We ourselves live in a culture which has brought itself, through questioning the phenomena rather than experiencing them, through "doubt" (honest or otherwise) leading to disbelief, to a *nihil*, a state of mind in which the phenomena have been emptied of divinity, emptied of life. Sun and moon have gone out. Modern scientific method has played its part, rejecting "value-judgments" as scientifically inadmissible. Our "revealed" world has given us water, ice, snow-crystals, steam, rivers and fountains, clouds and ocean, but science has given us an abstraction not a phenomenon. Life has delighted the soul with the rose, but science seeks to discover the nature of things by analysis, as if the rose could be found by removing its petals one by one. Trees and gardens, flowers and birds and all the living creatures science has reduced to chemistry instead of life, reflexes instead of feelings, a "big bang" for the divine creation of the world Keats calls "a vale of soul-making."

Technology – applying a materialist ideology derived from a science which has assumed, in our modern world, an authority which once belonged to God – has progressively built a world, beautiless and joyless, in the likeness of the materialist mentality which created it – machines, robots, computers – while treating the living world of animals and plants, earth itself and ultimately humanity also, as pieces of mechanism. Need we be surprised that the same mentality has produced cloning, genetic engineering, vivisection with all the rest of those loveless crimes against nature which science makes possible? Have too many changes that have destroyed the world in which "Everything that lives is Holy" already taken place for us to restore the old certainties and securities? Or can we, even now, raise our vision beyond the *nihil* to the unknown unknowable source, once called God, whether that source be in ourselves, or in and beyond the marvels of the phenomenal world, rediscover "that things which are seen were not made of things which do appear" – the ground of "faith"?

G. Gispert-Sauch

SOMETHING UNDERSTOOD

A question I have at times asked myself is why do I believe? Why do I opt for a religious outlook on life in this era when the secular or the agnostic seem so natural, so human, and so accepted by society? Why should I remain stuck in an attitude seemingly more appropriate to Antiquity or the Middle Ages than to the people who have lived through the Renaissance, the Enlightenment and the radical critique of religion of the socialist movement and the psychology of Freud? Are we, myself and my fellow believers at the end of the second millennium, fossils of the first? Are we the vestiges of an earlier stage in the evolution of the species, similar to the traces which the body conserves as reminders of an earlier biological stage now left behind?

An appeal to the wisdom of the past does not offer sufficient basis to justify the option of belief. Yet this is an option which even today millions of citizens of the modern world clearly make. Why do they? Is theirs a regression to the past made out of fear of the brave new world which threatens us? Is it a resistance to grow out of an infantile world? Or is it perhaps an option that promises power, a means to control the minds of others?

Faith and Humanism

To me, to believe is part of being a humanist. True faith cannot be an escape from life nor an evasion of the responsibility we all have of building a more humane world. Faith, or religion, is part of me because it links me more firmly to the totality of existence, with its cosmic, human and divine dimensions. Paradoxically, religious faith also protects the very roots of my freedom and personal existence.

Religion is said to derive from the root *religare*, to bind and therefore to keep together, to ensure wholeness. But authentic religion is not experienced as a bondage but as a source of freedom. In our Indian tradition religion is oriented to and colored by *moksa*. Its very goal is to liberate. It approaches that goal very gradually, through an educative process that at times does seem to involve bondage to the Law. But the very dynamism of religious faith makes us pass from dependence to socialization and to the deeper experience of freedom and personal integration.

One of the most striking expressions of faith in history, which has inspired many other believers in the second half of this millennium, was when Martin Luther, the rebel monk, standing erect in the Diet of Worms, shouted his defiant cry, "On this I stand and cannot believe otherwise." His defence of religion was a shout for freedom. He was effectively saying that because he was taking his stand on faith, he had a personal right and the freedom to withstand the power of the Pope himself, not to speak of the power of the Emperor. The religious obedience to God paradoxically liberated him from all slavery. If we do not root ourselves in the Absolute Value to whom we surrender, hopefully in love, we shall fall prey to human tyrannies, not least of which is the tyranny of our own subconscious or unconscious that control us and manifest themselves in self-centered caprices or in deep-rooted fears and anxieties.

Luther is also known for his slogan summarizing the message of St. Paul and the message of Jesus behind Paul: "Justification by Faith" and numberless books have been written on this theme. Without going into technical theological discussions, what Luther and much of the New Testament are telling us is that we are not authentic human beings unless we live by faith and in faith. Unless we remain rooted in God, the only Sovereign whose power liberates rather than enslaves us, we shall not be able to discover our own strength, or withstand tyrannies, religious or secular, that prevent us from becoming what we could be.

Faith As Religious Experience

Faith is one of the most fascinating words in the second Testament of the Bible and one most misunderstood. Too often faith is understood to signify just a religious dependence. Faith is also seen as a lower kind of religiosity, a dependence on authority more proper of children than of adults. Religions of faith, like Judaism, Christianity and Islam, are at times unfavorably contrasted with the oriental religions of experience like Hinduism, Buddhism or Taoism. Such contrasts are based on a derivative and often very imperfect understanding of the meaning of faith.

Faith is also seen by some to imply the acceptance of irrationality in our lives. It is believed that the call to faith is to shut the eyes and believe, when in fact the authentic tradition tells us to open our eyes and believe! The Buddha often said that he was not a teacher of the closed fist, but one with the open hand. Jesus also replied to the High Priest who questioned him, "I have always taught in public and not in secret" – which brought him a resounding slap on the cheek. The true masters called us to live by an enlightened faith, not by blind faith, and to live by the Spirit and not by the letter of the Law. Religious faith must be lived in the light. It cannot be irrational, even if it does not take its stand on human reason alone. This is one area in which fundamentalists of all hues need to grow in understanding: as long as they take a stand upon irrationality to defend their community or their traditions, they do no service to authentic religion, and offer no help for people to be liberated and free.

The authentic biblical tradition, (in the light of the contrast mentioned above, between religions of faith and those of experience), shows that faith itself is an experience. It has a mystical, a social and a personal dimension. When Abraham decides to root his existence and stake his future on a Promise coming to him from a Source he does not understand (*Genesis* 15:6), he transforms his whole life by changing his Center of reference. He sees himself, his world and his future in a new perspective. He now lives his existence within the Word of God so that his personal failures and the contradictions of life have no power over him. As Isaiah will say later, if we do not take a stand on God we do not stand at all (cf. *Isiah* 7:9 in the original Hebrew text).

Mystical, Social and Personal Dimensions

Thomas Aquinas sums up the mystical dimension of faith by saying that faith is *participatio quaedam in cognitione divina,* "a kind of participation in the divine knowledge." These words remind us of the *divya cakshuh* which the Lord Krishna granted to Arjuna to prepare him for the *Vishvarupa darsanam,* the universal vision. A divine eye, the light of faith or *lumen fidei* of the scholastics is, in the theological tradition, an affirmation of the presence of the Divine Spirit in the heart of the believer. Faith unites us with the Divine or Absolute Reality and this is the very fundamental teaching of St. John of the Cross. It is true that faith is related to the way of knowledge, still it goes well beyond all concepts. The Indian tradition has rightly insisted on this at least since the time of the *Upanishads: yato vaco nivartante, aprapya manasa saha ...* (*Taittiriya Upanishad* 2.6) – "From where words and mind come back empty-handed ..." The *Chandogya* and other *Upanishads* repeat the same: *na pravacanena, na medhaya, na bahusrutena* – "not by speech, not by intelligence, nor by much learning." In the union with the Divine Knower the believer, the person of faith, sees not only as God sees, but rather she or he partakes in the Divine Knowledge.

At a certain level, it is true, faith does find expression in credal statements which articulate in some form the deeper experiences not just of individual believers but of whole communities. These creeds of any religion are extremely rich in content if we are able to understand them within the historical context in which they were formulated and we open up the symbolic allusions which they encode. These creeds not only give meaning to past centuries and explain what was believed, but also strengthen and enlighten us for the present situation. St. Augustine spoke of the *rationes seminales,* seeds of understanding, which can grow afresh in each generation.

The community grows in its history out of the seeds of the past. The past continues to be with us and guides us into the future.

The expression of faith helps the community to find the sources of its unity. This is the social function of faith. The community realizes that it lives by a common vision, a vision which is not just a philosophy or a programme of life it has developed by human ingenuity, but the expression of a superior wisdom received as a gift from the deepest Source of existence. The community finds itself as sharing in one and the same mystical vision. The creed corrects not only the debilitating effects of doubt and hesitation on its individual members, but also the fissiparous tendencies which a heightened sense of individuality might develop in the social body of the believers. By faith they discover themselves as having not only one mind and one spirit, but also the experience of sharing within one body, one visible community.

Every community needs a point of reference. The more articulate it is, the more the members of the group are able to live in a sense of solidarity which does not conflict with authentic freedom. Every nation needs a Constitution, either written or kept up by oral tradition. Every society has its foundational charter. But no document as such is able by itself to ensure unity. A document expects and requires a personal assent, a free acceptance of faith on the part of each individual. Very specially, the religious creed, precisely because it deals with Transcendence, can never operate as a mere philosophical or legal text placed over and against the believer. The religious language is essentially symbolic, and the creed, therefore, calls for a bold and creative interpretation from within the believer's own historical context.

It is important therefore to distinguish the experience of faith from its expression. The expression may be necessary, for an experience that is never formulated tends to become extinct. A love that is never expressed dies of starvation. But the Creed, the expression is not the essence of faith. The essence is rather found in the mystical oneness between the religious person and the Divine Consciousness, in the fact that the subjectivity of the believer is integrated into the Divine or the Atman.

Faith is rich also in the measure in which it involves the noblest exercise of our humanity. Faith is not primarily a doctrine to be known. Faith is above all a commitment to a truth to be lived by all. It is therefore a commitment to all expressions of Truth. *Satyagraha* is another word for faith. Faith both builds on Truth and searches the wider expression of Truth. It involves the highest power of the human being, her or his capacity to love.

Faith and love are not really different. They are two words for the same basic attitude of adherence to the Whole, two aspects of the human response to the Divine Reality. Faith is commitment, and commitment means love. Faith indicates how love must be lived within the human condition of darkness and inborn uncertainty. Faith is a return to the Womb of Reality and to the whole human family in which we exist. This commitment springs from the core of our freedom. Faith is a free decision to live with a specific orientation to Truth and Goodness. This commitment liberates us from our deep-rooted selfishness, from the *avidya* that obscures our true belonging to the Divine cosmos. Faith is thus a protection from the disintegration of our being.

The Adventure Of Faith

The commitment of faith is a decision to walk firmly and with assurance towards the goal to which the whole world is called. Faith is not a "primitive" stage of human development, which metaphysics or science are destined to replace and show as unenlightened. Post-modernism has already showed up such rationalism as hollow and historically false. But the post-modern world is shattered and incapable of showing the way out of the present chaos. Only an enlightened faith, open to reason and the values of all the traditions and religions of humankind, can be a source of life, salvation and hope for our world. In our faith-vision we discover our place in the Mystery which is beyond name and form. In our faith we celebrate the values of our humanity including our limited reason. By faith we need to see ourselves not as separate monads struggling to preserve our little space in the galaxies of the universe, but see the whole of humanity, indeed all life, in many senses, as united in one bond, the Infinite Love that moves the stars.

Savyasaachi

THE SAGE FOREST

Thick forests cover the hilly region in central India, Bastar, which is home to a forest people the first inhabitants of the land who call themselves Koitors. They call their land *singarbhum* or the beauteous land.

Land came into being when Talurmuttee, Mother Earth, looked around at the vast expanse of water and wept, for until the waters cleared, and land emerged, there could be no life. To clear the water would be to clear the living space for all beings, to recover a sense of direction and bearings from the blank inscrutable surface of the waters. The creation story began thus. The story of creation is enacted every day – living space is cleared, every moment, within the forest, and every moment, Talurmuttee weeps to see it engulfed again. The cycle goes on endlessly.

Baba, the Koitor elder who lives on the outskirts of the Abujhmarh forest, concludes a part of Talurmuttee's tale (for it is a tale that has no beginning nor an end) and pauses to explain the Koitor way of "knowing." It is important to lose your way of understanding, he says, and then important to recover it again. And there is a difference between them – what you once understood and the new understanding. In the forest the way ahead is never

Photo courtesy P. K. De

clear, never certain to any degree, for the forest-scape is only a camouflage woven out of the co-presence of shades, colors, sounds – signals from the living world of plant and animal, bringing together the tangible and the intangible, the empirical forest in its closeness and the idea of the whole in its symbolism.

Baba tries to explain and simplify the way of the forest thus: "If you are a boatman and rowing with skill and confidence, the idea that you are moving across the sheet of water in a chosen direction gives you a sense of certainty. You are sure you will reach the shore. But that is not so when you are holding on to a log with the idea of remaining afloat. The flow of water moves you along – but the idea absorbing you is that of remaining afloat, of not drowning, and knowing that in time the log will drift you to the shore." In the latter case which Baba describes, the log, the water, the wind and you are in a togetherness, each recognizing the other's presence – a togetherness and a recognition that one might call faith.

So also in the forest. The forest presses upon the body and the mind; it pelts the senses with a myriad signals. It is not easy to find direction or make out patterns of "objective" reliability within the mindscape. Yet, having lost one's way in the dense vegetation, one can find it again as every pore of the body and the very innermost mind processes the symbols and signals that press upon them. One recovers one's bearings and the sense of the whole is restored. Limbs, eyes, ears, leaves, twigs, the human and the non-human, are all in synchronous understanding without words or maps or charts.

This essay attempts to understand this process of forgetting and recovering memory, of coming to wholeness and of the difference between the "modern" world's verifiable, predictable certainties, and Baba's faith.

In order to live and survive in a forest it is important that man and other living beings recognize each other's presence and keep to their respective paths. On occasions when two or more paths cross each other there is the possibility of losing one's way because in the forest, unmarked and inscrutable, the way ahead is indistinguishable from the way back.

Panic is futile when lost. Panic is our insecure response to the uncharted space of the forest that does not yield its secrets to our objective analyses. What is needed now is not control but rest. The individual has to come to rest, and confront the forest from within, and when this dramatic moment comes, it initiates the process of recovering one's bearings.

But before that there is the forest to acknowledge. To begin with, what one sees does not synchronize with what one hears, and no sense can be made of either. Between the two – the visual and the auditory cognitions – lies the forest-in-hiding, camouflaged, secret, full of multiple symbols and a symbol of itself. The many sounds and sights tell that it is alive and animate – it watches with many eyes, speaks with many voices. They speak of the interwoven and intermeshed nature of its being and of the beings to which it is home. Gradually the eye begins to distinguish the faintest shades of the landscape. Yet, even as the process of differentiation begins there comes an experience of the dissolving of boundaries between self and forest, between human and non-human nature. In place of the earlier mental certainties, what emerges is an awareness of the totality of the forest and of the self-in-the-forest. The dissolution of boundaries restores a sense of unity, a sense of the whole.

And yet one resists. Possessed by the forest in this way, apprehension and fear grips the mind – for now, no-thing is distinguishable from no other thing. The presence of the forest is perceptible all along the contours of the body. Enveloped by a multiplicity of symbols, the human body is permeated by non-human nature. Every pore opens up to receive the "presence" of the forest and consequently there is loss of the presence of mind and therefore, a loss of the sense of direction along which to move. It is now, under these circumstances, that one may move to a point of rest. One may now begin to recognize the difference as well as interrelatedness between human and non-human nature. Sounds generated from the body become distinguishable from those generated from the forest. This primary differentiation takes place when a convergence between what is heard and what is seen begins again. Without the differentiation the mind can conceive neither relatedness nor wholeness. It is therefore an important aspect of the act of faith, for in acknowledging the other, it recovers the importance of all living beings in the world. The world has many centers and each is true. This is crucial for the recovery of the sense of direction as it reveals the truth that man is not the center of the world.

To make the world intelligible one needs to remember and to forget. This dialectical relationship between memory and forgetting shapes the imagination. But it is important to identify what must be remembered and what needs to be forgotten, only then will the relation between the tangible and intangible aspects of everyday life and of the larger social and historical context become intelligible. It is a similar process and a crucial one through which one arrives at the understanding of both, the distinction and the relationship, between the knowledge of faith and the knowledge of predictable certainties.

The forest cannot be deciphered unless one learns to know it like the owl does. The owl flies by night, turning its head all the way, each side. To turn the vision through one hundred and eighty degrees is to recognize the divergence of symbols even while recovering their convergence. Within vision and within hearing a space is made for all the senses. One learns to "see" through every sense, through skin and tongue, through eyes, ears and nose. The perception becomes total. Where earlier, the camouflage of the forest caused a loss of perspective, there now emerges a complex of multiple perspectives. One loses, and in losing, learns and recovers something else. Such recovering is not possible without loss. One loses perspective and that is faith. One recovers multiple perspectives, and that too is faith, as is the miracle that the forest which held the threat of death is now intelligibly a space for life and living. The forest is a camouflage of symbols but the camouflage is also a host of symbols.

When, as a hunter, one steps out of his familiar everyday path he pursues the path of another living being. He must therefore recognize the odor, pathways and pattern of the animal within the camouflage of the forest, in order to spot it and take aim. With the help of the keen senses of sight and hearing he must track down and identify animals by their pug marks, by the arrangement of fallen leaves, the grass that gives cover, by marks on trees, and so on. Hunting is premised on a study of the forest and is directed towards the following of existing pathways and constructing of new ones. During hunting one learns the way in which memory and forgetting together clear the social space and restore the presence of living beings, and in the process the significance of non-human nature. It draws attention to the "whole" namely, the living forest.

Such a process of dissolution and recovery defines the framework for all material culture. The idea of a "dwelling" partakes of this process. For instance, in the construction of a house, the material and tangible aspect of a dwelling is derived from an understanding of the relation between forest materials such as mud, bamboo, wood, elephant grass, the character of space, the presence of godly beings, and so on. Such understanding underlies the process of construction. The first step is to select and clear a site in the forest. Then mud is dug out from the ground nearby. It is mixed with water and kneaded by people. Subsequently, mud blocks are carried over to build the house. The walls are rectangular and the pyramidal roof is thatched with elephant grass. All other conditions remaining the same, the house can last over a generation if looked after. It is likely to dissolve, if left unattended, into its original elements, pushed by the forest regenerating across seasons. In the process, the passage of time is redefined and acquires a dream-like quality. Each object, each being, each space moves to its own time, framed in its own rhythm of dissolution. So too, not all spaces are alike and homogenous. Each has a quality of its own. For this reason, not any place can be a site for the construction of a house. Indeed, dwelling has an ideal (ideational) dimension as well.

How are we to understand the dissolution of the house? The dissolution of the material tangible aspect of a dwelling restores the unity of the forest-living-space. The house becomes forest; the forest returns. The return of the forest is also a return to the point of origins, when there was only the forest and human life was submerged in it. This return is simultaneously a recovery of the ideal dimension of the dwelling, namely, its relation to the origins. The sense of the passage of time for those enveloped by the forest of symbols acquires a dream-like quality. Like dreams, the forest is self-active. Time, like dreams and forgetting, dissolves and regenerates itself. This is privileged time. It makes space for a clearing, to show the metaphysical depth of everyday life. It also points to the fact that the dialogue between dissolution and recovery is no different from the dialogue between forgetting and memory. Without it the sense of meaning in everyday life dissolves, this in turn undermines faith and the ground for being in the world.

Underlying a "clearing" in the forest is the relation between two contrary aspects of dwelling which run in contiguity in time and space, namely, the work of man and the work of nature. Each has a tangible, material dimension, and an ideal dimension. The relation between these two defines faith as the ground for being in the world; its rupture undermines faith. Together, they highlight the significance of self-activity for the mutualness of man and nature. For instance, self-activity determines the longevity of materials. The duration of time over which materials dissolve and the forest regenerates, frames the time of self-activity as also its meaning for being in the world. It determines life cycles of different durations and highlights the unity of the empirical and the ideal aspects of the multiple symbols that go to make a living space. It is the contrast between different durations that unfolds the dialogical exchange of memory with forgetting and layers the sense of the passage of time.

Is the question of faith linked to the recovery of memory and does forgetting threaten the sense of certainty? Conversely, does the lapse of memory undermine faith and is remembering the basis for a sense of certainty?

A clearing is a bounded open space and it is a basic requirement for life. To make a clearing is a continuing activity undertaken from birth to death, and it constitutes the life process. To cut is therefore a necessary activity for without it no clearings can be made. However, there are different ways of cutting a social boundary. Their character is determined by the way in which they allow for the regeneration and recovery of the origins. The method of clearing determines the pattern of memory and forgetting. To be unable to forget, and to remember everything or to forget all and remember nothing both result in violence and aggression, for in either case the relations between things in the world are destroyed. To let a relation be unfragmented or undamaged one needs both to remember and to forget. It is necessary to cut away, to forget, to make a clearing. It is also necessary to remember the space to recover and inhabit it. Without both forgetting and remembering, there is no clearing and therefore no possibility of social life and of hope.

Individuals as thinking beings are continuously engaged in making sense of the world in which they live. This effort is primarily concerned with "making a clearing" and understanding the large universe to which they belong. The imagination, harnessed in the process, is strained to creatively understand the "whole" from which everyday things derive their meaning and significance. Such an understanding strives to bring together fragments, to heal ruptures and to recover the fabric of life from its damages and injuries. This journey of the imagination is within oneself; it moves along pathways that are perhaps not yet discovered.

The capacity of the imagination to hold the sense of the whole perhaps lies in the possibility of losing and recovering one's way in the world. This is the basis for faith. In contrast, the sense of the logical and rationally predictable outcome is concerned with a fragment without letting the imagination work out the "whole" to which it belongs. Faith restores the sense of belonging. In contrast the sense of predictable certainty reinforces alienation, so long as it is not contained within the imagination of the larger whole. The loss of the sense of the whole undermines faith. One manifestation of this is the loss of the sense of direction and of one's bearings. Faith is the quality of relations among things in the world. In the course of living life, the basic nature of things themselves grow clearer in the light of these relations. The linear path rowed by the boatman does not necessarily bring understanding of the whole. But the faith of the man afloat on the log understands the limited path of the former also, within the whole.

One of the important concerns of industrial development and of modern life is about predictability of human effort and of events in nature. It is the guarantee that with the predictability of empirical science man can reach the moon, explore the depths of the sea, unveil the mysteries of the so-called unconscious mind and thereby bring light into the lives of people. However, it does nothing to generate faith. It gives no confidence to cope with the crises of everyday life, nor prepare the ground for continuity or the well-being of all.

There is an experience of certainty in the accuracy with which the human spacecraft landed on the moon, or the atom bombs fell on Nagasaki and Hiroshima. The process has converted everything including man himself into an instrument for refashioning the world, for re-affirming his claim for centrality in it. However, not only has the continuity of life been undermined, but more importantly the human condition of being itself has been left exposed and uncared for. The capacity to recover and regenerate, which are the constitutive forces in man and nature, have been ignored and damaged. Although man can reach the moon with some predictability, his being in the world is fragmented and damaged. In losing our sense of the whole, we have lost faith.

Our living in this world is what Baba speaks of as the crossing of the river. We can cross this river in a warship, alienated from the waters, controlling them and continue our journey through our skills and objective rational knowledge. Or we can make this crossing with the river, with our supporting log of wood, one with wood, water and air, one with the world that has submerged in the water. We can make this crossing with faith. Certainties do not create space for faith, but faith brings us to an unshakable certainty. Faith is that quality which is the relation among all things, that brings us to a sense of our location, bearing and direction, and to a deep knowing of who we are.

Karen Armstrong

REINVENTING OUR SACRED

There is certainly a crisis of faith in the modern world. People complain that they find the truths of religion incredible, that science has disproved the existence of a personal creator God, and that the laws of the various faiths seem arbitrary and archaic. There is also a void at the heart of the modern experience, a widespread anomie, and disappointment that modernity has not proved to be the panacea that everybody expected. Scientific rationalism has achieved marvels. We are now able to view our planet from outer space. We have an entirely new perspective on life. There have been tremendous advances in medicine and technology so that, at least in the privileged sector of the world, people are able to live longer, healthier and more comfortable lives. But there is also loneliness in our megacities, isolation and discontent. In their quest for transcendent experience, some are turning to drugs or to extremist forms of faith to convince themselves that life has some essential meaning.

Part of the problem is that we now tend to equate faith with believing certain propositions, whereas faith is a virtue. We human beings, unlike animals, fall very easily into despair. Unlike dogs, who do not seem to agonize about the canine condition, the fate of dogs in other parts of the world, or the possibility of afterlife, men and women are constantly plagued by these existential questions. We are also so constructed that we have always experienced a transcendent dimension of mundane life, that goes beyond our normal perceptions, and which we can never wholly define. We have called this transcendence many things – God, Nirvana, Brahman, *mana* or the Sacred – but however we choose to interpret it, it has been a fact of human life. In the eighteenth and nineteenth centuries, many Western people assumed that science would answer all our questions about the cosmos, but that has not proved to be the case. Science has uncovered still greater mysteries – so much so that some physicists, who adhere to no conventional faith, are evolving what can be seen as a new type of religious discourse, that holds us in an attitude of awe and wonder before the dark world of uncreated reality.

In fact, we need to experience this transcendence which puts us in touch with the deeper currents of existence and, in consequence, makes us feel more fully alive. If we no longer find it in a mosque, temple, synagogue, or church, we will seek it elsewhere: in sex, drugs, music, theatre or even sport. That is why as soon as men and women became recognizably human, they began to create religions at the same time and for the same reasons as they started to produce works of art, which evoked in them this sense of transcendent awe and an inchoate conviction that despite all the depressing evidence to the contrary, life has some ultimate value and significance, even though they were never able to find rational justification for such a belief. In the pre-modern world, therefore, people in all cultures recognized two different means of arriving at truth. One was *mythos* or myth, which relied on the intuitive insights of art and religion. It was an attempt to express the inexpressible, and it was understood that it could not be explained rationally. Nor could it help us in the pragmatic organization of our lives. Instead, it provided us with that sense of transcendent meaning which human beings seem to need if their activities are to have value and point. The other mode of knowledge was *logos*, or discursive reason. We need *logos* when we want to function efficiently in this world; *logos* is the source of science and politics. Unlike *mythos*, it has to be seen to be effective and to make logical sense.

Mythos and *logos* were complementary. They could not be confused with one another, without becoming perverted. Neither was superior to the other. Humans needed both modes of thought. Each had its particular area of competence. *Mythos* could not give advice about the political structure of society, nor about the best way to farm the land. It was no use looking to mythology for practical information or concrete facts. Its insights were more elusive. They were not achieved by systematic rational thought, but through the intuitive techniques of contemplation and the aesthetic rituals of the cult. The words "mysticism" and "myth" both derive from the Greek *musteion*, to close the mouth or the eyes. They are both associated with silence and obscurity, not the lucid clarity of articulate discourse. It is also a matter of scholarly debate which came first: the mythical narrative (such as the story of Demeter and Persephone) or the cult associated with it, so inseparable were they felt to be. Without the rites of prayer and liturgy, the myths of religion can make no sense. But *logos* also had its limitations. As any scientist will be the first to admit, it cannot address ultimate questions that exceed the evidence of our senses. Nor can it console us when confronted with the ubiquitous tragedies of life. When we are in despair over the death of a child or the killing fields of Kossovo, we do not want a rational discussion, but prefer to read a poem, listen to great music, or find somebody to give us a wordless hug. Faced with such catastrophe, reason is silent and has literally nothing to say.

The advent of secular modernity, however, broke the old partnership of *mythos* and *logos*. The achievements of scientific rationalism have been so spectacular that by the nineteenth century, *mythos* was beginning to be discredited, and *logos* was seen as the only avenue to truth. Today in popular parlance, a "myth" is something that is not true, that did not happen. To make their faith respectable in this world, people have often tried to turn the myths of their tradition into *logoi* and prove them scientifically. This has been one of the main preoccupations of Christian fundamentalists. In other faiths, which do not place such a high value on belief or doctrine as Christianity, there has been a tendency to discard rituals that seem irrational and which can serve no practical function. Muslim and Jewish fundamentalists have all used the *mythoi* of religion as blueprints for political action, often with disastrous results. Any attempt to turn *mythoi* into *logoi* – modes of perception that were hitherto kept separate – will produce bad science, bad politics and bad religion.

In 1882, the German philosopher Friedrich Nietzsche declared that God was dead. In *The Gay Science*, he imagined a madman running into the marketplace crying: "I seek God! I seek God!" When the supercilious bystanders asked him where he thought God had gone – had he taken a vacation, perhaps, or emigrated – the madman simply glared at them. "Where has God gone?" he demanded, "I will tell you. We have killed him, you and I. We are all his murderers." In a profound sense, Nietzsche was right. By neglecting the rituals of faith and the contemplative disciplines of prayer, many modern men and women had killed in themselves the sense of the divine. God is not a fact, like the atom, whose objective existence we can demonstrate and accept notionally. The experience of the sacred has to be evoked by the intuitive and cultic practices of religion, just as we cultivate an aesthetic appreciation of great art. Nobody who has not immersed himself or herself in the Western musical tradition, for example, has a hope of appreciating the last quartets of Beethoven. Without prayer and ritual, the myths of religion seem arbitrary and nonsensical. They need to be conveyed into the hearts of worshippers by the aesthetic disciplines of faith, just as for most of us a musical score is incomprehensible until it has been translated into sound by a skilled musician.

In the contemporary world, people often feel that they are not prepared to live a life of faith until they have satisfied themselves intellectually of its objective truth. This is good scientific practice: first you establish a principle, then you apply it. But all the great masters of the spiritual life say that in religion the reverse is true. It is only when you live in a certain way and open your heart and mind to the interior life that you begin to receive intimations of sacred transcendence. Only then will you be convinced that God,

Brahman or Nirvana is a Reality, even though you cannot explain this faith rationally. One of the chief disciplines of faith that produce this "God-consciousness" is compassion. All the great world religions insist that the divine is not simply transcendent and "out there," but is enshrined in every single human being with whom we come in contact. If religion should be considered an art form, rather than as a statement of scientifically verifiable fact, it differs from art in that it must have an ethical dimension. One of the chief functions of religion – at its best – has been to curb the murderous egotism that often seeks the destruction of others in order to ensure its own survival. Human beings are among the only animals that kill their own kind, and all the faiths have devised rituals that remind us of the fact that every man and woman – even those who do not belong to our ethnic, religious, or ideological group – must be treated with the same respect that we accord to God.

We must learn to recover our sense of the divine by rediscovering the symbolic power of *mythos*. That is not to say that we must cling blindly to the forms of the past. Religious people have always been highly inventive in their attempts to interpret the doctrines and rituals of their tradition in a way that speaks to their particular modernity. But since religion is an art form, we should expend on our theological writing and on our liturgy the same creative care and energy that we would devote to writing a poem or a symphony. There should be no weary and lazy reliance upon old insights in our attempt to help people to evoke a sense of the divine in a radically altered world. It is a project of the greatest urgency. The horrors of Auschwitz, Bosnia, Kossovo and East Timor show what happens when all sense of sacredness is lost.

V. S. Naipaul

NOT AMONG THE BELIEVERS

G iven the theme of this volume, with what expectations did
one approach V. S. Naipaul for his views? So distant from
the subject and yet so near, his own staunch position of disbelief
enabled the writer to observe a specific section of believers, with a
detachment that was almost clinical. Or was it?

In this interview with Sima Sharma he is alert against any
infection of evangelism. And yet, even so, he admits to "a sense
of wonder" and finally, yes, "I believe in myself." That, he
stands by. Alas, the common English usage often blurs the
distinction between faith and belief. So, what about the faith of
the disbeliever?

Sima Sharma: Sir Vidia, your views, your intuitions and your
    observations on our relationship with the world as
    individuals have been always fascinating. I am here to seek
    your views about the issues of religious belief and also faith.

Sir V. S. Naipaul: I have been misunderstood at various times and
    I wish to make it clear that I don't wish to offend anyone
    in his belief and in his religion. I'm speaking only because
    I've been asked, and I'm speaking very, very personally. I do

not want to interfere or appear to be less than reverent to anyone. I'm speaking historically.

SS Thank you. As a reader I've always felt deeply moved by your sense of places, where layer upon layer of memories cover the ground and wield a power of their own. I wonder, would you say that places have a religious or extra-material quality of their own? Perhaps religions, some if not all, arise from the soil. Can they ever be transplanted on to other soils? Can they be crossbred across cultures, towards something radically new and more universal?

VSN I think your question is the concern of someone who has grown up in a place where the basic religion is the earth religion: a religion which has come out of the earth. This is true of India. By that I mean, I'm contrasting that with the revealed religions of the world amongst which the two principal ones are Christianity and Islam.

Your question then about whether they can be transplanted – well, I think these revealed religions certainly can be transplanted. But these two revealed religions are quite different from each other. Christianity is not like Islam, except in one particular: both religions encourage social ideas and these are very valuable, as those of charity and brotherhood.

But Christianity was not a racial religion. In fact, when it triumphed, it triumphed over the principally racial religion of Rome. For a thousand years the Romans and their successors had honored Jupiter – Jupiter the greatest and the best. That is the way they put up their altars of dedication and it was the religion of the Roman people – their exclusive religion. Christianity did not have that kind of exclusiveness.

Islam, the other one, is an Arab religion. It imposes all kinds of imperialism on its converts. It gives them Arab names: it tells them that their history before Islam came into their own country is quite worthless and should be eradicated. You see good examples of this happening in Afghanistan and Pakistan, where no one is working harder to eradicate the historical past.

This is contrary to what is happening in the rest of the world where we wish to know more about the past, to honor the past, for we wish to find out about what we come from. And the same thing is happening in countries like Malaysia and Indonesia. However, part of the tension is their wanting to eradicate the past. That is the tension in a place like Indonesia. The people of Aceh, the people in Sumatra, are fanatically purist. They are converts but think the rest of the country is not moving along fast enough – still honoring the Buddhist shrines, still respecting the past. So they decide that. And the convert, having learnt to despise his land, his own old religion and his language, has to look to the language of Arabia, and at the monuments of Arabia. It is all in Arabia. That is his sacred place.

SS You're talking of a kind of dislocation which takes place within a location ... but ...

VSN You see, there can be no meeting of a religion which thinks like that and one which deals in matters of private speculation, conscience and so forth. So the idea of the interfaith dialogue is nonsense.

SS What does one mean by religion then? After all no religion or culture is ever pure. I mean, they all evolve in interaction.

VSN Well, you tell me what you mean by religion?

SS I was thinking there are two points: heaven and earth. Walking down the lanes, a city is a very different thing from what one sees looking out from a skyscraper. But both are equally true. One tries to reunite the two. At the very individual level too, there is a meeting, perhaps not in the bylanes of history and culture but in the higher aspects of being human. It doesn't matter to me what religion you belong to, but something else does matter, something which is beyond the label of race, creed, etc., that you carry.

VSN I have no time for that. I know what you say is very lyrical, poetic, but I do not think like that. I've given you my very practical historical view about earth religions that have come from a country and then the revealed religions.

Also, I don't think the revealed religions have much to offer the world now, any more. What they had to offer has been offered. I think Christianity in fact came as the religion of the dark age – a religion of darkness. It abolished the humanism of the classical world and reigning for fifteen hundred years, it was a world of extreme darkness. The Renaissance came only with the rediscovery of the classical humane past in Europe. There's another thing about Christianity that came to the ancient world. I find it impossible to understand all those sects, the passions, the theologies. That's probably because it took so much from very far away things of the classical world. This is why it is opaque to me.

Somehow, inspite of all of that, with the coming of the Renaissance, it gave birth to good ideas about humanity, society and things like that. But that work has been done. I don't think there is anything more to do. I think Christianity has nothing more to offer. In England, religion is really no more than an aspect of social life, self-conscious manners. And I think in Islam, you now see this fundamentalism which is pure destructiveness.

So, I think, as people we have to look more to ourselves, our own ideas of goodness. We don't have to depend on other religions, on other systems or systems outside ourselves. We have made use of what has been offered to us by our past. And now we have to move on to be more self-supporting.

SS Individually? Each in our own way of thinking?

VSN Yes, yes, in profound thoughts. I don't think we want any group ideas. They tend to be so bogus, don't they?

SS Perhaps you're speaking of what should be. But when you

observe what is happening on the ground, even over the past ten years in our contemporary world – it's not at all benign – isn't there a movement towards a more organized and powerful system of belief? Could this tide be a kind of new religion?

VSN No, I think it is varied. In a place like England, religion is almost dead. It is absurdity what passes as religion. In the backward countries in Europe, it is essentially a kind of magic. The idea of a religious faith in a person sounds wonderful, but it really means they believe in magic.

SS So what lies ahead?

VSN Things have to change and evolve all the time. It is absurd for these revealed religions to think that they are eternal. They are not eternal. They are historical events. True.

SS But the quest is eternal. Wouldn't you say that it just refuses to go away, inspite of so much discouragement?

VSN There is no quest. There is only an expression of wonder. There is no quest. People say they are looking for truth. I don't understand the meaning of those words. How am I looking for truth? I think it means I'm a very vain person. I'm saying pretty words. I'm trying to give myself a little lift.

SS Yes, but one is also talking about compassion and being able to understand people over here and across the world.

VSN Well I'm saying that it has to be done privately. You don't need faith for that. That is where the trouble comes. And you get all these crankish groups, specially in a place like the United States – all these crank religions – they say they are religions too. I think the cults in America have to do with their kind of vanity, and the element of vanity must not be discounted. If you examine these cults, many of them seem quite alright folk but they are very vain and boastful people. Their cults are an aspect of their boastfulness, and they also have an element of aggression. You start wearing your costume, your uniform, and be aggressive. People go around with their hair done in a certain way. They are expressing their aggression. I don't think we should find beauty in things like that.

This word, religion has been misused so much. Please understand that Livy, writing his history of Rome – you know, a man two thousand years ago at the beginning of the Christian era, roughly that cross-over period – said that the Romans were the most religious people of the world which was the reason for their success. By that he meant they always consulted their gods. They always did their sacrifice, never performed actions before testing the auguries, having the priest consider things before they were done. They never acted just like that. They had a great sense of awe, Livy was saying that. And then, of course, at that very time their religion was being replaced by something else.

SS Do you think something like that is happening today? An excess of some kind of world-view is perhaps being corrected mid-course?

VSN I don't think so.

SS You've travelled across cultures and across beliefs. Have you never felt that there is anything which an extra rationalist agenda can offer?

VSN No!

SS So it is within the material-rationalist paradigm then, that we have to seek our responsibilities and our answers?

VSN Not our answers. There really are no answers. We just have to deal in the sense of wonder. That's good enough. And take to heart what we've picked up from the revealed religions – Islam with its idea of brotherhood, Christianity with its idea of doing unto others as you would have others doing unto you. A piece of great idea. These are perfectly good things.

SS You are pointing time and again to the sense of wonder and that's a thread which runs not only through spiritual literature, literary writings, poetry but also science. In that sense of wonder is perhaps a source and an indicator of where one ought to go, perhaps where convergence can take place of many conflicting and fragmenting trends today.

VSN I think the idea of convergence is wrong. Why should people converge? Once we share certain ideas of humanity and we respect rationality, I think we all will be able to get along.

SS Is history logical then? Logical progression of things that happened before and then continue....

VSN I don't know if it is a logical progression. All I mean is that x creates y, and y creates z. I think they follow like that. I don't mean there is any logical sequence as when you are coming to a goal, you know. An event is an event.

SS But there are consequences ...

VSN There are consequences. I think you have to be very careful talking about interfaith and convergence. When you are faced with barbarism here – and there are many places in the world now – you must recognize it for what it is. Please do not try to find points of contact with barbarism.

SS How does one cope with barbarism?

VSN I think we try to kill them. There are some people of whom you can only see as so wicked, they have so little regard for me as a human being, that the only way you can deal with them is by destroying them.

SS You can destroy people but not ideas and intents. They live on.

VSN I'm not thinking of that. I'm thinking of a man who is a barbarian, who has no regard for me, for my mind, my emotions, my thoughts. I am not going to try to convert him. I only wish to get rid of him.

SS That's only one person. But unfortunately the idea lives on. It's not that one can really cancel that.

VSN You just have to fight that bad idea. You must not try to accommodate a bad idea.

SS No, never, I'm precisely against just this – the accommodating of bad ideas – and would like to eliminate these properly. Would you say that the destruction of the wicked alone can help or is there another way of really changing the bad idea into something else?

VSN No, no. That's not for me to do. That's for other countries and other cultures to do. I mean I can't deal with that.

SS Yes, I understand.

VSN I can only write about the spectacle, see the spectacle and report on what I find. I can see how it occurs. I can see bad thought leading to bad ideas, leading to bad behavior, to wicked behavior. I'm not going to try to say, we can improve it by doing x, y, and z.

SS So one separates the good and the bad within society, and then either one eliminates or is eliminated through the countering of opposite forces.

VSN Yes, I think one has to. Yes.

SS I think I understand your stand. We hear so much about conflicts that are just. Wars which are just. Just interventions. There has always been a heavy ethical and political agenda that religions have carried. They have not always been a pure quest for the soul or God. That is the political and social aspect. And yet there is also the inner journey ...

VSN I don't know about those inner journeys. I cannot sympathize with them at all. I just deal with my own sense of wonder. That's enough for me.

SS What about other kinds of belief? Like, belief in yourself?

VSN Yes, I had believed in myself. I don't know where I got it from. It's as though I had a kind of stubbornness, because I've no earthly reason to believe in myself. I had no earthly reason to think that operating in a new and hostile society – trying to be a writer here in the 1950s – that I'd make any headway. It was very hard to live here. I just went on.

SS But inspite of all that you say, isn't there a certain loneliness which one feels in having to work things out entirely on one's own and within oneself?

VSN Yes. There is nothing one can do about it.

SS It's an utter sense of being alone. And yet it is not a peaceful sense and does not feel right. For truly, you are implicated in just everything that happens. Whether you like it or not, you are indeed your brother's keeper.

VSN Loneliness doesn't worry me and I think certain cultures are lonelier than others. I think the loneliness of people in this country is extraordinary. The loneliness of people in India is probably not as extreme.

I think what happens is, that as you get older, you start seeing the end of things for yourself. Many people's reaction to that is to start to believe in some kind of deep permanence in themselves. Instead of accepting with great relief that they are coming to the end, they wish to fight it by erecting some belief. It is some kind of vanity or fear. My own feeling is I'll be happy to go. You see I'm different from people who wish to live forever. I'm aware of the end and I would accept it as a release.

Raimon Panikkar

FAITH: A CONSTITUTIVE HUMAN DIMENSION

> If you do not believe,
> you will not exist.[1]
> Isaiah VII, 91

The problem, to begin with, is that contemporary human experience – followed, generally with delay, by philosophers – clearly shows that Man, when deprived of faith, does not know how to bear the weight of an existence torn by internal struggles, nor can he sustain the continual demand to surmount the tensions created by communal life. Deprived of faith, Man collapses. From a phenomenological point of view, one could say that Man is being "designed" to function in the realm of faith.

Note:
Some elements of style such as the use of capital letters and lower case are peculiar to Panikkar, which we have retained. On the use of the word Man to mean human beings, we quote Panikkar's own words "... Man means the androgynous human being and not the male element which has hitherto monopolized it ... it is not that the masculine stands for the whole Man, but that the whole man has allowed this untoward domination by the male. The solution is not juxtaposition (he/she etc.) but integration." – Ed.

Believe that You May Understand

Such a fact is plausible not only phenomenologically but also within traditional philosophy. Man, as a conscious being, can only be founded in truth – and ultimately be – if, in some way or other, he can see, intuit, comprehend, believe that his existential situation has a foundation that is not himself. Without this awareness his existence is mutilated. A plant lives as long as sap runs in its stalk; Man needs that ontic sap, which gives him his being, runs up to his head and heart. Any philosophy uses similar arguments. Hinduism and buddhism would say empirical Man is not his own foundation – be it symbolized by fullness, nothingness or any other pertinent symbol. Faith is precisely that x in Man which makes possible the "recognition" of the foundation, for by it Man is united (at least intentionally) to this foundation. A human being cannot attain his destiny if he does not "recognize" the foundation of his being. Now faith is precisely what manifests this foundation. Without faith Man cannot live an authentic human life.

A passage from the *Bhagavad Gita* seems to express what I wish to say: just as there are three kinds of Man according to classical Indian anthropology, there are three types of faith, one corresponding to each of these fundamental human types. "Man is made by faith: As the faith so the Man."[2] Without now investigating the notion of *Śraddhā*[3] (faith) – which originally signified the theandric condition essential to the efficacy of the sacrifice – it can be said that our thesis is in harmony with the spirit of the indic religions[4] and in general with every religion.[5]

We may go further: The mediaeval christian said, *Crede ut intelligas* (Believe that you may understand).[6] This expression does not indicate just the ontological priority of faith with respect to reason, i.e. the existential situation in which Man cannot understand if he does not believe. It is something more, and it is this intuition I wish to comment upon.[7]

Believe that You May Be

Faith is not only necessary in order to understand, but also to reach full humanity, to be. In other words, faith is a constitutive human dimension. By faith Man is distinguished from other beings. But precisely because of this, faith is a human characteristic that unites mankind. Thus faith is not the privilege of some individuals or the monopoly of certain defined groups, however large their membership. Faith is not a superfluous luxury, but an anthropological dimension of the full human being on earth.[8]

We maintain that if creatureliness can be said to be simple relation to God, to the Source, or whatever name we give the foundation of beings, faith is another name for the ontological relation to this mystery that characterizes Man, distinguishing him from all other beings. If beings as such are nothing but this relation (the creature neither is nor has its foundation in itself), Man is that unique being whose rapport with the foundation becomes the ontological link that constitutes him as Man.

In saying "relation" to "God," I am not assuming a kind of merely "private" link with an exclusivistic and anthropomorphic God, but the constitutive radical relativity of all things, so that this link is not a solitary "relation" to an only transcendent "God" but a relation of solidarity with the whole of Reality. The traditional way of expressing this view would be to say that the "theological virtues" are also cosmological ones or, in a word, cosmotheandric. Faith, Hope and Love are not only vertical, but also horizontal.

If religion (from *religare*: to tie again, to re-link) is what links Man to his foundation, faith is what frees him from mere cosmic existence, from being simply a thing. Freedom arises in this opening to, or rupture from, his subjection to the realm of objects. By this freedom Man is placed at the heart of the personal trinitarian relations, sharing in the creative act of the Divine. The relation between God and Man can in no way be free unless there is freedom within the Godhead itself and Man is somehow integrated into the intra-divine free-play. This is what the idea of the Trinity, in any of its forms, is saying.[9]

It may be important to add that this thesis, although expressed in a particular language, need not be linked to a single philosophy or religious tradition. It claims to be as valid for a buddhist as for one who calls himself an atheist. The meaning of words depends not simply upon the semantic expression, but also upon a whole collection of cultural connections that should not obscure our central theme or turn us aside from it. On the other hand, I may be excused from not undertaking excursions into other cultural worlds and not utilizing other frames of reference. All terminology is just the concrete objectification of a cultural system. A discourse in totally abstract terms, i.e., lacking any cultural connections or reference, is impossible. The reader may find it easier to understand what I am saying if he translates my words into those of his own personal frame of reference.

The Consequences

This thesis has important consequences. It provides the key to one of the most important problems of our time: the encounter of religions. In other words, it delivers us from the impasse in which the science of religions currently finds itself. It suggests the astonishing possibility that the encounter of religions might be a religious dialogue – even at the level of faith – rather than a mere rational dispute. It may also serve to free religion from its exclusivistic aspects, its frequent sectarian character and from an archaic unilateralism incompatible with the process of openness in which humanity is engaged. Recognizing faith as an anthropological dimension situates the encounter between people on a fully human plane and does not exclude religion from the dialogue.[10] In a human encounter worthy of the name, it is not enough that Men recognize their brotherhood in shared biological functions or elemental needs while raising barriers when it is a question of a deeper embrace.

One cannot put faith in parenthesis any more than one can bracket reason when truly human understanding is at stake, unless one would castrate Man and render him not only infertile but monstrous. Faith is the foundation and guarantee of human relations. Banishing it would inevitably condemn us to solipsism by destroying the last possible foundation for a path to any transcendence, beginning with that transcendence which allows ourselves to "go out" of ourselves and meet our fellow-beings without alienation.

Understood in this way, faith is also a condition for love and guarantees its creativity. Faith cannot be ignored in considering the deepest realities of human life; it is part of a fully human existence on earth. Every profound human encounter in which faith is left to one side can only appear hypocritical to someone who does not think he has faith, for in such a meeting, the so-called non-believer does not meet the believer on the same level if the latter has bracketed his faith; what is ultimate and definitive for the first is only penultimate and provisional for the second, and vice versa. For the Man of faith, there is no real encounter because by putting his faith in brackets he shuts away precisely what the "non-believer" would like to put on the table.

Further, we can suggest that it is in and by faith that the believer "communicates" and fraternizes with the Man who calls himself a non-believer. Removed from this deep level of faith, human fraternity becomes an infra-human communication of the biological order or even an artificial contact, like a computer that always gives the same results when fed the same data. Reason does not get us out of this situation because it divides, decides and distinguishes, but does not unite.

For several centuries, western Man has been indoctrinated that his humanity (and consequently his universality) was grounded in reason. The effort to discard theology, and faith along with it – to reduce the latter to a corner in humanity's sacristy so that the real human encounter can be realized in the domain of pure reason, of true and uncontaminated philosophy – has characterized "modern" philosophy since Descartes. According to this view, faith would be a privilege gratuitously given by God to the few. Faith would then separate Men while reason would unite them and provide the possibility for universal human communication. Theologies differ, it is said, precisely because they are based on something "more than human." As a result, rational philosophy becomes the universal science and following the judgments of reason appears the only way to attain, if not a celestial, at least a terrestrial paradise. "Two and two make four anywhere" is the popular summary of this attitude. "Religion divides people while reason unites them" is its sociological translation. As the only source of universal knowledge, rational philosophy is thus opposed to theology, which it construes as merely exegesis of gratuitous propositions.

However, the recent historical and philosophical evolution has put Man, mostly western Man, on guard against a naive rationalistic optimism. Today, after two world wars, a cold war and so many atrocious wars before our own eyes, after the failure of idealism and the ensuing chaos of philosophy, faced with an almost world-wide revolution of an entire generation against another, our confidence in reason has been thoroughly shaken. We are actually beginning to suspect that "two and two do not make four" except in a purely ideal and abstract realm. It is the revolt of life, of the concrete, which refuses to be imprisoned or paralyzed in reason's formalism. Two roses and two violets make four flowers, to be sure; but completely different from two lilies and two jasmines, although these are also four flowers. Is love for a mother plus love for God the same as love for a car plus love for a garden? Reality cannot be so simply manipulated.

Faced with the non-reasonable situation of the world, the defenders of "pure reason" advance the argument of contamination. The failure of reason, they say, is due to something for which reason itself is not responsible: in itself reason is infallible, but in operation, desires, passions and feelings mutilate it, render it impotent. The argument, however, is not convincing. First of all, it begs the question and demands a far greater leap of logic than that of the famous, and so often misunderstood, "ontological argument." In fact, it represents, a jump from the "real order," which we experience as fallible and non-rational, to the "ideal order" of pure reason by postulating the infallibility of reason. Further, the argument is unconvincing because, even if it were to prove anything, it would be useless: a reason that is theoretically infallible and practically impotent cannot help us. We are not concerned with knowing the theoretical rights of "pure" reason, but with what can actually guide Man. Reason verifies (falsifies) and criticizes; it does not discover and guide. Perhaps we have been seduced by a distorted definition of Man, by removing its most salient element, animality, and so converting Man into a "logical" being.[11] In addition, logos is often interpreted in an excessively rationalistic fashion. But I am not interested in attacking reason.

The word "reason" does not need to stand only for a merely Cartesian reason, and today this word includes the entire mediaeval meaning of intellect and even more.

The urgency of our problematic, however, lies in another direction, whose importance and gravity we discover when we confront it. One of the most striking phenomena of our age is atheism. The various manifestations of contemporary atheism generally coincide with denying the object of religious faith: such atheism denies the christian affirmation of the existence of God, rejects the theistic affirmation of transcendence, etc. Today, somebody is often declared an unbeliever because he refuses to objectivize his faith and does not wish to limit the possibilities of his existence by being recognized as a member of a part of humanity – more or less great – but nevertheless only a part. We could say that a certain monopoly of faith on the part of some groups has taken from him the possibility of believing.[12]

At this point the gravity of our theme appears: Faith cannot be recovered because it was never lost. It is purified because its content is questioned as being ever inadequate.

We might mention in passing two connected problems: the "loss of faith" and "conversion." Does one really lose faith or is one simply abandoning certain beliefs? Does faith disappear and does Man flee the light? We refer to the so-called great crisis of faith that besets our epoch. Have the catholics of post-Vatican II lost their "faith" because they no longer believe what their ancestors held to be the case? Have the neo-marxists and euro-communists to lose their identity because they no longer agree with orthodox party lines? And conversion: is it a real change of faith or a return to an interiority enabling us to discover what we, in an inadequate or unconscious way, already believed? Would not every conversion be a gnosis, a knowing, a metanoia, a change of mind, which reveals to us the true name or the authentic belief of what we already believed?

We refer to the great traumas caused by conversion into other religious "creeds" that no longer need imply a rupture from an abjuration of the previous tradition. Has a hindu becoming christian to denounce all his hindu past? Or has a christian becoming buddhist to forego what he still believes is valid in the christian tradition? Or has an indonesian becoming muslim to sponsor the arab cause? Has conversion necessarily to entail alienation? Should we then not distinguish between faith and belief?[13]

THE THREE INSTANCES OF FAITH

To elaborate a little further, I wish to bring to mind two conceptions of faith that illustrate this inexhaustible problematic.[14]

The first conception, founded on the primacy of an essentialistic conception of Truth, leads one to identify faith with orthodoxy, i.e., with correct doctrine properly formulated. The second insists on the moral character of the religious act, based on the supremacy of the Good, and consequently leads one to identify faith with orthopoiesis, (right-doing) with the attitude and moral deportment that lead Man to his destiny. It should be clear by now that we have taken the Aristotelian concepts "poiesis" and "praxis" as relevant for our distinctions. By the first we understand human activity whose result falls on the external object to which the act is directed: in the second, the act reverts on the agent himself and transforms him. If the first risks "dogmatism," the second skirts "moralism." These two interpretations may not be false but only one-sided. We offer the notion of faith as orthopraxis (right-acting).

Orthopraxis does not center faith in another particular faculty of Man, but links it to his very being seen as act. If Man as Man is a religious being, his religion cannot be a sect, his religiousness cannot be one element among others. Rather his religion must be based on this free movement that penetrates the totality of his being, rejoining his most profound existence to its source. Faith is what gives him this freedom.

Man possesses intelligence and will. He rushes forward drawn toward the Truth and the Good. But he is not exhausted there, or, better said, these primordial activities spring from an even more radical source: his very being, and his being is act. Human life is not exhausted either in the thought process or in extrinsic constructions: Man is much more than a spectator or constructor of the world. Above all he is an actor; fundamentally he enacts himself through his capacity – not exhausted by his *facere* (to do) – to embrace his *agere* (to act) as well. His activity is not simply poiesis, but above all praxis. Herein lies the meaning of the sacred action that all religions recognize: the horizon of orthopraxis.

Through faith Man becomes himself; in other words, he is saved, completed, attains his fullness, obtains liberation, his final end, by whatever name he may call it.

Religions do not claim primarily to provide each a doctrine or a technique. They claim to save Man, i.e., to liberate him or, in other words, to open for him the way to the fullness of his being, whatever this fullness may be. When this end is interpreted as an intellectual vision, the doctrinal aspect comes to the fore. If, on the other hand, it is seen as a reward for a life, for moral conduct, the practical values have the primacy. But in both cases, they presuppose that human fullness consists in acquiring this value that lies at the center of human finality.

Orthopraxis illuminates a fact prior to all doctrine and all deportment: Man should reach his goal and fullness, however we may interpret these expressions.

Praxis is that human activity which modifies and fashions not only Man's exterior existence but also the interior dimension of his life. The effect of praxis is part of Man's very being: it is the salvific activity par excellence. Within a certain metaphysical framework, praxis is that activity which actualizes the potentiality of the human being. "Work out your salvation with diligence," said Gautama just before his death.

The quintessence of faith, then, reflects this aspect of Man that moves him toward fullness, this dimension by which Man is not closed up in his present state but open to perfection, to his goal or destiny, according to the schema one adopts. Faith is not fundamentally the adhesion to a doctrine or an ethic. Rather, it is manifest as an act that opens to us the possibility of perfection, permitting us to attain to what we are not yet. The notion of orthopraxis does not eliminate the possibility of erroneous actions, but it excludes the possibility of interpreting them only in terms of doctrine or morality.

Every action that leads to the perfection of Man in his concrete existential situation, every action that leads Man to his realization, is authentic praxis, way to salvation.

FAITH AS HUMAN INVARIANT

Theological Consideration

Beyond orthodoxy and orthopoiesis, we can still ask what comprises the real essence of faith.

Having posed the theological problem in this way, we are led to seek the structure of faith belonging to the very constitution of Man. Now a critique of an exclusivistic faith should not cause us to go to the other extreme and defend a universality that excludes all discrimination and difference.

On earth Man is not perfect: He is neither fully Man nor truly God (realized, risen, ...). He has the capacity to become what he must be in order to realize his destiny; in fact, he must actualize it concretely. The first capacity we call "faith," the second "act of faith."

Philosophical Reflection

We seek something in Man that links him to transcendence, brings him to his end (Absolute, God, Nothingness or whatever); in other words something that makes progress possible toward what Man is not yet, the bridge connecting him with his destiny. This "something" must be sufficiently ample and universal to constitute the foundation of salvation for Man as Man. It must justify our affirmation that the very fact of being human means that Man has the real possibility of attaining the end proper to him. This end — however we may characterize it — is what we have called salvation.

Evidently, this "something" cannot belong to the purely doctrinal order since the world of concepts depends upon the possibilities offered by the different cultures through which it is expressed. In fact there is no universal culture in either time or space.

And a concept is meaningful, and hence valid, only where it has been conceived.

This fundamental "something" we seek can only be found as a constitutive dimension rooted in the very existence of Man. Our task is to try to describe it, and we say "describe" because, in speaking of a fundamental human dimension, we lack any external overview for a rigorous definition.

We could describe faith as existential openness toward transcendence or, if this seems too loaded, more simply as existential openness. This openness implies a bottomless capacity to be filled without closing. Were it to close, it would cease to be faith. The openness is always to a *plus ultra*, to an ever farther, which we may call transcendence and in a certain sense transcendental.

One is open to what one is not or, rather, to what one has not yet become. Real openness means the possibility of being: openness to Being. It implies a capacity to be ever more and more filled, an "in-finite" receptivity, because Man is not "finished," finite. Man is open because he is not closed, he is not complete because he is itinerant, not definite, not "finished," incomplete. The existential openness of faith represents Man's capacity for his non-finitude, that is, his in-finity. No person considers himself as finished, as having exhausted the possibilities of becoming. The opening of which we speak is constitutive of the human being, the other side of what we call contingency. This latter appears when we look backwards, to our foundation, thus discovering that we do not have in and of ourselves the ground of our own existence. The former, i.e., the existential opening, appears when we look forward, towards the goal, the end, the transcendent, etc., and discover that we are not complete.

We should not affirm *a priori* that all religions say the same. An important branch of the buddhist tradition will object to the language I have just used. And in fact the buddhist insight obliges us to go a step further, towards a kind of metaontology. Hardly any other religious tradition has more forcefully under-scored the fact that we are not, so much so that it will say that we should not surreptitiously intercalate a "yet." The way to *nirvāna* implies precisely the total openness without qualification.

Recognizing Man's openness means admitting he is not God, not finished, absolute, definitive. It means admitting there is something in him that may grow. The openness of faith is Man's capacity to proceed towards his fullness.

This openness is not primordially a capacity of the intelligence as the faculty of the infinite, but rather an openness we call existential to indicate that it does not exclusively belong to the realms of intellect or will, but to a prior level given in the very existence of Man. Only the naked existential order, previous to intellect and will, offers the desired universality.

Thanks to this dimension of faith, Man recognizes that he is not finished, he needs completion; better, he needs definite aid to attain the goal. Thanks to faith, Man discovers his indigence. Faith is precisely the base underpinning both human precariousness and the possibility of overcoming it. Further, Man's grandeur and his supreme dignity are expressed by faith, since its existential openness does not signify merely need but complementarily indicates an unlimited capacity for growth. Finally it represents a much firmer foundation than human autonomy or self-sufficiency, and expresses the supreme ontic richness possible; we recognize that no "human" or limited value whatsoever can fill it.

Existential anxiety, modern gnoseological atheism and certain social ideologies today are various manifestations of this fundamental attitude of faith that is not satisfied with anything closed, limited, finished. Human dignity resides precisely in the anthropological dimension of faith: Man is an ever open, infinite being.

Faith is the foundation of freedom. Without faith Man would not, could not be free; he would have neither the constitutive ambiguity that permits decision, nor the spontaneity necessary for the human act to go beyond – not against – the dialectical possibilities given in the data. True freedom does not consist in manipulating possibilities but in creating them.

The openness of faith is a constitutive openness. It cannot be closed; it is finite, neither limited nor limitable. Faith is like a hole in the human being that is never filled, saturated, or turned into a kind of substantivity that would represent the supreme religious blasphemy and sever Man from any relation with the infinite. Through this hole he reaches the infinite (cf. *śunyata*).

It is essential to faith to be a powerless capacity, an ontological thirst that cannot be quenched, an anthropological aspiration that cannot be satisfied and that – if it could – would annihilate Man by destroying this constitutive tension that thrusts him ever toward the Absolute (whatever we call it: God, nothing, Man, society, future). Faith is constitutive of humanity's itinerant condition.

Faith relates to Man's inquisitive structure. He asks because he does not know yet, but – and this makes him truly an inquiring being – he also asks because he knows that he does not know yet and because he knows that in knowing he will obtain not only the answer but that on which the answer is based. The question also provides the frame within which the answer can appear as an answer: Ontically the answer is contained in the question. The question, then, is nothing other than the ontological condition for the answer. Consequently every question is an inquiry about God and Man. No question ever obtains an adequate response, since at bottom every question is about the infinite. We speak, of course, of human questioning and not of mere asking for information. Each authentic question is a human incursion into nothingness.[15]

Until now more philosophical importance has been given to the ontological than to the ontic and, as a result, faith has been considered a response rather than a question. According to this understanding, faith belongs to those who give the correct (doctrinal) answers or those who at least act morally.

The essence of faith seems to me to lie in the question rather than in the answer, in the inquisitive stance, in the desire rather than in the concrete response one gives. Faith is more the existential "container" than the intellectual content of "that thing" we try to describe. It belongs not only to those who respond correctly, but to all who authentically seek, desire, love, wish – to those of "good will." The proper realm of faith is orthopraxis, the right actions Men believe they must perform in order to be what they believe they must be.

We have, moreover, distinguished between faith and the act

of faith. The latter is the free response to faith, is Man's reaction to this capacity that instills in him the thirst for the Absolute; it is his decision to respond to the possibilities presented him in daily life or in the particularly serious moments of his existence.

If faith is an existential opening, a vital questioning, the act of faith is equally an existential response. It is, however, part of the perfection of the act of faith that it also possesses an intellectual and volitional aspect. The human response to the thirst for perfection, the desire for transcendence, the free reaction to what several schools see as an appeal from transcendence – this constitutes the act of faith.

Everybody "has" faith, every human being is endowed with this constitutive dimension; but no one is forced to live *ex fide*, out of faith or from faith. Such a life characterizes the "just Man." In other words faith is not the act of faith; the latter can be positive or negative and of different degrees of purity and intensity. Our conception of faith does not imply that Man cannot "sin" against it or perform a negative act of faith, but these are aspects of the problematic we do not need to investigate further here.[16]

This article is an abridged and partial version of a study by the author published in french in 1966 and in english in 1979.

Notes

1. This text has been widely commented by the christian tradition. Cf. Augustinus *Epistula* 120, 1, 3 (Patrologia Latina 33, 453), *Sermo* 43, VI, 7 (Patrologia Latina 38, 257), *Sermo* 118, 2; 126, 1, 1; etc.
2. *Bhagavad Gītā* XVII, 3; cf. also IV, 39; XVII, 17; etc.
3. Cf. *Brhadāraṇyaka Upaniṣad* III, 9, 21. Cf. K. L. Seshagiri Rao, *The Concept of Śraddhā* (Delhi: M. Banarsidass 1971 [1974]), and P. Hacker, *"Sraddha," Wiener Zeitschpift Kunde Sud-Ost Asiens* VIII (1963).
4. Cf. the little known text of the *Kṛṣṇa Yajurveda.* "Faith envelops the Gods, faith envelops the entire universe. For this offering I am augmenting this faith, mother of desires." *Taittirīya Brāhmaṇa* II, 8, 8, 8. Or again the entire chapter 6 of the *Tripurā-rahasya* dedicated to faith: "... faith is the ultimate resort of the whole world ... Everyone is able to communicate with the other because he believes the other ... faith is the way to attain the ultimate good ..." Cf. A. U. Vasavada translation (Varanasi: Chowkhamba Sanskrit Studies, vol. L, 1965).

5. Cf. G. Widengren, "Mythe et foi à la lumière de la phénoménologie religieuse," *Mythe et Foi*, edited by E. Castelli (Paris: Aubier, 1966), pp. 315-32.

6. Cf. E. Gilson, *Reason and Revelation in the Middle Ages* (New York: Scribner's Sons, 1954).

7. Cf. a characteristic text by Aristotles: "Whoever wishes to understand must believe" (*Against the Sophists*, II, 2:165 b 2 [although one could translate: "he who wants to learn has to trust," later tradition has interpreted it in the former sense]).

8. It is worth pointing out in this context the traditional idea that loss of faith is, in a certain sense, *contra naturam* (Cf. D. Thomas, *Summa Theologiae*, Part II-II, quaestio 10, article 1 ad 1.).

9. Cf. R. Panikkar, *The Trinity and the Religious Experience of Man* (London: Darton, Longman & Todd and Maryknoll, NY: Orbis Books, 1973), esp. pp. 40 ff.

10. The religious encounter, we have said time and again, is neither a private meeting of isolated individuals nor a meeting of abstract generalities, but the concrete meeting in time and space, among living persons, each of whom carries in a more or less complete and conscious way the burden of an entire tradition.

11. The famous aristotelian dictum of Man as "animale rationale" (a rational animal) means, in fact, "Man is the only animal whom [nature] has endowed with *logos*, the gift of speech," (Aristotle, *Politics* I, 2, 1253-9 ff.; cf. VII, 13, 1332 b 5), which is a totally different matter.

12. "Today the faculty of faith lies hidden in innumerable human beings," is the beginning of K. Jasper's important study *Der philosophische Glaube angesichts der Offenbarung* (München: Piper, 1963) p. 7. (*Philosophical Faith and Revelation*, New York: Harper and Row, 1967, p. xxv.)

13. Cf. R. Panikkar, *The Intrareligious Dialogue* (New York: Paulist Press, revised edition, 1999). Chapter III. Cf. also W. C. Smith, *Belief and History* (Charlottesville, Va.: University Press of Virginia, 1977), speaking on faith rather than belief as "the fundamental religious category."

14. Cf. J. Mouroux, *Je crois en toi* (Paris: Cerf, 1949), english translation: *I Believe: the Personal Structure of Faith* (New York: Sheed and Ward, 1959). Cf. also T. Izutsu, *The Concept of Belief in Islamic Theology* (Tokyo: Keio Institute, 1965).

15. Cf. R. Panikkar, *El silencio del Buddha* (Madrid: Siruela, 1996), pp. 187 ff.

16. This last paragraph seems necessary as a response to the query that if everybody has faith, nobody has it, or the worry that failure, tragedy, sin, damnation and the like are not possible. They are indeed possible precisely because the act of faith is a free act.

Shabda – Sound

Ghulam Rasool Santosh

THE REVERBERATING IMAGE

When light withdraws colors recede –
Light reverts into sound again
Of their own the throbs go
Leading Sound to soundless state,
Color I possess will not last long,
How long can a painter paint?

G. R. Santosh (trans. K. L. Kaul)

Always and in almost all cultures, there are some who understand the universe as a region of consciousness, not of space. In the direct experience of such seers, the man-nature separation does not exist. Nor is there separation between thought and experience or between mind and matter. Their synoptic vision regards the world of senses, as neither a veil nor gross matter but one in the spirit with the highest Nature and Divinity.

Ghulam Rasool Santosh (1929-97) was born in a land ripe with such gift of sight and quest – the Srinagar valley, framed in snowcapped peaks holding a tradition rich with Kashmir's saints,

We are grateful to Mrs. Santosh (Toshi) for the paintings and writings of G. R. Santosh reproduced in this volume and for the biographical details of her husband.

sufis and Shaiva Darshan. Poetry came to Santosh first, and writing in Urdu and Kashmiri, he became an acclaimed poet in his early twenties. Then came Love, no passing dream, but as the girl whose very name Santosh, he made his own. But it was art that claimed him in its entirety. His quest for the unmanifest behind the manifest led him to the symbol that stands for cosmic harmony – the fusion of the masculine and the feminine of Tantra, Shiva and Shakti. The painter and seeker found himself and the cosmic self in line, color, light and love, to invoke the holy spirit.

– Editor

SPARSHA   AIR

ROOPA   LIGHT

Tanum Trayate iti Tantrah

"That which activates the body (*sarira*) by the exhalation and inhalation (*prana apana*) of breath is tantra.

The universal mind (*Brahman*) manifests itself by its own will and when transformed in an artist's mind becomes self-creative. The individual mind of an artist has the potential to transform the visual concept into the materialized creative expression: a work of art.

The immanent universal mind (*Brahman*) is beyond causation and the individual mind is subject to the laws of time and space. And, when the individual (*jivatma*) comprehends the universal (*Paramatma*), it becomes *That*.

The individual mind is the embodiment of unending thoughts, perceiving objective reality directly and indirectly. The mind of an artist is conditioned and activated by continuity of thought, thereby rendering the creative expression self-consistent. The formless subjective experience becomes, through the process of creation and re-creation in the framework of time and space, a work of art.

Indian tradition is based on the universal concept of the ultimate reality manifesting itself in a myriad shapes and forms in time and space. My own self is preoccupied with the same universal concept. Therefore, I am He (*soham*). My paintings are based on the male-and-female concept of Shiva and Shakti and, therefore, construed as Tantra. It is not just the man and woman concept. Any semblance in my paintings in this respect is symbolical, but my stress is on the more fundamental male-female (*Shiva-Shakti*, *purusha-prakriti*) principle with its infinite connotation with all the pervasive light emanating from the objective reality.

To me painting is a necessary, normal activity, no more special than any of my other activities. It is an integral part of my 'being,' my *svabhava*, my *karma*."

– Santosh, 1978

RASA   WATER

GANDHA   EARTH

"My canvas represents a projection of *sunya*, the Void, which is incalculable in time and dimension; in fine, which is *anadi* and *anant*. The surrounding dark oceans in terms of which you describe the borders of my canvas are the ever unfathomable, unreachable, infinite aspects of the fundamental Creative Force which lies beyond the pale of wisdom, thought and imagination. The canvas itself therefore is symbolic, as it portrays the omnipresence of the Infinite in the finite.

By *Prakash Vimarsha*, as the Kashmir Trika philosophy puts it, the vibrant but invisible force acquires *roopa* and *nirakar* manifests itself as *aakar*. It is a process of self-illumination. Taking you to the birth of my painting, this desire for manifestation is represented by *mooladhara*, a hollow, or an illuminated circle in a focal point, in each and every one of my canvases. The source of light does not exist somewhere outside the image, as it did for the Impressionists, for instance, but within it, as light which is appearance is merely a transformation of sound. The concept is not my own, but it is the quintessence of my heritage of thousands of years. It is the heritage of this land. That may perhaps explain why you find a response to my painting in your blood channel rather than merely in your brain. That should also account for the inadequacy of the norms. However, the image which, as you have correctly described, is very symmetrical and arises around the *Mooladhara Chakra* or self-luminous circle in terms of prominent female anatomy which I call Shakti and a symbol of Shiva which is the male attribute of the same, the image resting sometimes on the latter symbol itself. Being preeminently a native concept with its ramifications in every conceivable motion of thought and deed in our life, I have had to go past the deviating centuries into our unperturbed tradition of iconography and *yantras*, in search of fulfilment and satisfaction."

– Santosh
(From a dialogue between K. L. Kaul and Santosh)

E. C. G. Sudarshan

My RESEARCH AS MY *SADHANA*

When I was about twelve I read portions of the college textbook of physics that my elder brother was using. In it I came across the formula for the period of swing of a simple pendulum. It appeared very remarkable to me that by using mathematical equations of motion, one could compute the period and then verify its validity in the laboratory, or on the playground! This wonder of theoretical physics – to be able to predict the values of physical quantities using pen and paper – continues to be a source of wonderment and joy. Such are the isolated but significant episodes that shape our life's path. I went on to study physics at the university and later at research institutions; but I owe my commitment to the simple pendulum.

The amazing thing in science is that the theoretical insights are verified experimentally. Experience is the final arbiter, however elegant the theory. Experiments, however, cannot be usefully carried out without some theoretical framework. And as in other contexts, a benevolent mentor and worthy co-workers are very desirable. But despite what other people say or feel, ultimately you have to arrive at your own conclusions. I was privileged to work with a great teacher and guide for my doctoral work. In turn, I have been a guide to a score and ten students, some of whom are smarter than me, and in turn act as my mentors on occasion.

These observations, gleaned from my journey as a scientist, are intended to show the roles of mentor, theoretician and experimenter in the pursuit of pure science. All of them are essential. They appear as common elements and fundamental to the modes of exploration and discovery which the human mind follows through various disciplines of enquiry. In addition, there is the element of subjectivity of the individual who is pursuing the enquiry. You are happy to have others agree with you but they may not, and you have to make your own decision. Moreover, in creative science all objective assessments are subservient again to your subjective assessment of those making the assessment.

Such relative principles – of the subjective and the objective, of theory and experience, of mentor, philosopher and practitioner – obtain in the domain of spiritual discipline also in a similar way. You may read or listen to others, develop a cosmology in your inner space, but ultimately the truth has to be validated in experience. And the final judgment is your own. I was privileged to spend extended periods in discussion with a most outstanding and affectionate person, who used to say "I tell you, don't follow anyone, don't listen to anyone!" We pointed out that in that case we should disregard his own words. He resolved this paradox by saying that as long as it was "another person" you were hearing, you do not follow it unless you hear your own self tell you to do so.

There is this anecdote about a severely ill patient being declared dead by a well qualified physician. Subsequently two attendants put his body on a stretcher to take it to the mortuary. On the way the patient wakes up and asks the stretcher-bearers why they are taking him to the mortuary. They tell him "Who knows better whether you are alive or dead: you, or the doctor?" People sometimes react to someone else's spiritual path in the same way: Who knows better, you or the others?

In general, objective assessment is held to be of such paramount value in science that it often seems to say "Don't trust yourself but trust others." However, when science operates in the domain of insight and creativity, and functions beyond the usual mind, the scientist steers alone, with subjective experience directing the course of his work. On the other hand, the experimental validation of theoretical structures is something that spiritual disciplines also demand. In turn, these experiences, in either discipline, enlarge and extend your theoretical structure.

Then again, in scientific creativity as also for spiritual insights, while you can recall a time when you did not know, the moment the experience arrives, it comes not as a strange one but something that feels totally familiar. It fits into your experiential fabric. Your own feelings say that it was not you who brought about the insight but that it happened in an *impersonal* domain. You do not feel proud; the only discernible reactions are awe, gratitude and joy. It is for the sake of such opportunities for this wonderful life-experience that in addition to my own research, I guide research students. Ultimately it is their own discovery. The fact that they have been guided towards it or have heard or read about it, does not diminish the glory of the experience. And when I have a second or third such opportunity, they don't appear to be disparate to me, instead I have a sense of the same extraordinary functioning continuing without interruption. For most of us who have been enthralled by a sunset, each time we witness it, it is the same as the first, not different. Time and chronology take on a new texture. And this functioning is joyful and totally familiar.

It is the same sense of joyous wonder that fills you each time on seeing a newborn baby, especially so if it is your own. You feel privileged to be in on creation, and all your knowledge of physiology and embryology detracts not a whit from the wonder. No less is the wonder that comes upon seeing a new grandchild. When I held my first grandson in my arms, the joy was indescribable. And again the same experience returns with subsequent grandchildren! It is the same modality of awareness functioning without a break and comes from the same, somehow familiar and impersonal, domain.

These peak experiences, embodying a singular sense of wonder are after all accessible in our lives. Yet, why is it that this realm is not acknowledged, and not pursued? Partly because people have been told that such pursuits are unscientific or unsuited to a rational intellectual person. And like the mortuary attendants, they believe what they are told. Needless to say, not every path is suited for everyone; it is here that a mentor or friend can be of help as in any other pursuit. However, there is one other serious worry for the rational scientist. Would the spiritual path detract from scientific or intellectual activity? Would one get "blissed out"? Would there not be such a risk?

Well-wishers and good friends have often asked me "You are a pretty good scientist: Why do you waste your time with all this nonsense?" (One self-proclaimed intellectual even wrote an article psychoanalyzing me in absentia. He "forgot" to send me a copy or discuss it with me in person though we meet often.) How can I explain such "waste of time"? Some days ago I was at a Yoga conference and spent four precious days there which I could have used to pursue "science." But what my colleagues may not know is that I got to spend time with an aeronautical engineering professor, a chemistry professor, a physics professor, a psychiatrist and a neurosurgeon, each of whom I hold in great esteem. Most of my bemused fellow scientists are too busy for such gatherings: they are afraid of others and even afraid of themselves.

My purpose here has been to emphasize the experimental aspect of the spiritual path. True, there are many excellent scientists who have no interest in spiritual experience. A good friend who is a great scientist once told me that he had invested too much in his world-view and that he dare not embark on a path that may change it. I respect his choice. The majority of the disapproving tribe are, however, intellectually lazy.

While every path cannot be for everyone, I am amazed and sorry that most of the world's intellectuals neither know the beauties of the "nine-point circle" of a triangle nor the wonderful world of analytic functions – things worthy of exploration. In the will to explore there are of course choices which one has to make, just as I had to choose physics instead of microbiology. So also there are different paths in spiritual exploration.

To summarize: Why the spiritual path? Simply because it is a source of joy and wonder, in the same way that the life of research leads the scientist to the source of joy. Do we trust every self-proclaimed spiritual adept? No, but then we do not trust every self-proclaimed scientist either. Does the spiritual path detract from your scientific creativity? Not that I have noticed.

In fact, scientific research at its best, is also a spiritual *sadhana*. Perhaps one who recognizes this is on the spiritual path, whether he admits it or not! I hail from a region where there is a lot of water and boats are aplenty. One lesson taught to us was that if you put your two feet on two different boats you must be careful. That advice may be relevant in the present context also.

I died mineral
and turned plant
Died a plant
to turn sentient
Died a beast
to wear human clothes
So when by dying
did I grow less?
Again from manhood
I must die,
and once again
released,
soar through
the sky

And here as well
I must lose place
Everything passes.
But His face

                    Rumi

You that can turn scales into feathers,
sea water to blood, caterpillars to butterflies
metamorphose our species; awaken in us the
powers that we need to survive the deep crisis
and evolve into more aeons of our solar journey.
Awaken in us a sense of who we truly are:
tiny ephemeral blossoms on the Tree of Life. Make
the purposes and destiny that free our own
purpose and destiny.

                    John Seed

Philip Sheldrake

PLACE, PERSON AND THE SACRED

A "sense of place" is nowadays an increasingly important theme in Western writing on cultural history, philosophy, architectural theory, anthropology, ecology and human geography. Reflections about "place" are also common in contemporary English and American novels. This concern for a sense of place is closely associated with the search for meaning and human identity and not surprisingly is beginning to interest those who study contemporary spirituality.

In this article I want to reflect briefly on why "place" is a spiritual issue. I inevitably write from within my British and Christian cultural and religious contexts. So what follows reflects personal experience and presuppositions although I hope that I have been able to write in ways that will resonate beyond the boundaries of these worlds.

A Crisis of Place?

I want to suggest that we in the West are experiencing a crisis of "place." Part of this crisis is cultural and at its root lies a decline in traditional value systems – religious, ethical and social. The resulting fragmentation tends to inhibit moral or social consensus.

This new context is often labelled "postmodernity." Essentially, two world wars, the Holocaust, Hiroshima and the threat of nuclear annihilation withered the optimism that had once characterized the "modern" period since the European Enlightenment and Industrial Revolution. Despite today's rapid technological developments, it is no longer possible to believe in the absolute inevitability of progress or in the capability of reason alone to solve every problem. People are increasingly suspicious of any universal framework of meaning that claims to possess "the truth" in some total way.

Thus, our spiritual experience of "place" at present has sometimes been characterized as wandering in a wasteland, among the ruins of former theories of meaning. Within the uncertainties of a postmodern world, a culture of individual choice implying the freedom to choose from the widest possible range tends to push aside social idealism as the goal towards which people strive. Even the increasing interest in spirituality is often individualistic and privatized. The question is whether we are also in a "place" of transition towards an eventual recovery of some kind of collective meaning. Interestingly, the great French intellectual, the late Michel de Certeau, offered a more spiritual and hopeful interpretation of the postmodern experience. For him, we are on a kind of pilgrimage that in a way parallels the mystical tradition. Like the mystic we experience dissatisfaction with a fixed or final definition of things and are driven onwards in a movement of perpetual departure. Each of us "with the certainty of what is lacking, knows of every place and object that it is not that, one cannot stay there nor be content with that."[1]

Another dimension of the contemporary crisis of place is social. The social geographer Anne Buttimer suggests that it is essential to have "place identity" but that since the Second World War we have de-emphasized place for the sake of economic values such as mobility, centralization or rationalization. The global relativity of space dissolves the reality of place. "The skyscrapers, airports, freeways and other stereotypical components of modern landscapes – are they not the sacred symbols of a civilization that has deified reach and derided home?"[2]

The modern city celebrates and facilitates mobility at the expense of settlement and "place." However, without a sense of place there is no centering of the human spirit. In an increasingly placeless culture we have become "standardized, removable, replaceable, easily transported and transferred from one location to another."[3] If there is a sense of place, it is predominantly a private one in the face of suspicions about the outer, public world.

For us westerners, the city as a humanly constructed "landscape" is a paradigm of this privatization of place. Cities are the monuments of collective consciousness; living symbols of our ideals. Medieval European cities were part of their surrounding countryside. The division between urban and rural life was not hard and fast. It is not surprising that in the decoration of the great medieval cathedrals, such as Chartres just outside Paris, the rural imagery of the seasons and harvesting was common. "The countryside" was not a detached place for leisure. In contrast, today's western cities are largely disconnected from surrounding place and food production. Their citizens are global consumers.

The monumental architecture that characterizes many of today's cities stands neither for the value of individual persons, nor for intimate relationships, nor again for any focused sense of community. Rather, such architecture speaks the language of size, money and power. Modern commercial buildings, such as the Canary Wharf tower in the London Docklands development, exist in brooding isolation rather than in relationship to anywhere else. City developments in recent decades frequently lack proper centers that express the whole life of the community. There are few examples of architecturally designed open public spaces, equivalent to the piazzas of Florence or other Italian Renaissance cities. The absence of such design forces us back into our own worlds behind defences rather than invite us out into shared, humane, meeting places. New domestic ghettos are increasingly protected against sterile public space that is no longer respected but abandoned to violence and vandalism. Unfortunately, the Christian spiritual tradition, historically, has not always been a positive influence because (following St. Augustine) it tended to separate the outer (worldly) from the inner (spiritual) space.

Cities reflect and affect the quality of human relationships. In the context of urban development, we cannot separate functional, ethical and spiritual questions. So, do our built environments support relationships that express the best of the human spirit? Environments that conflict with human proportion lack either intimacy or glory, and undermine our identities. If place is to be sacred, our designs must affirm the sacredness of people as well as our capacity for community and transcendence. Too often our urban places are not like this because we have built nothing into them that is really precious to us. In the cities of an earlier age, the cathedral fulfilled that function. It was at the same time an image of God and a symbol of the ideals of the citizens. The Prince of Wales' recent article, "A Vision for the Millennium," contained a plea for us to think more deeply about the spiritual basis of human existence. Part of this, surely, must be a radical renewal of the basis of urban living.

The Human Experience of Place

Why is a sense of place so important? When I lived in Cambridge, there was a permanent display in King's College Chapel that explained the purpose of the building for modern secular tourists. It began with the sentence: "We exist not only in the world but in an image or picture of the world." In other words, we all have world-views that are conditioned by different experiences and assumptions (including religious or spiritual beliefs). These determine our values and behavior. The architecture of King's College Chapel expresses a medieval Christian view of the cosmos. World-views have changed radically since then, even for Christians, and continue to be challenged by advances in cosmology and quantum physics.

The point is that the "world" is not simply a neutral collection of raw data but is something we interpret and to which we give meaning. In other words, it is a "place." "Place" is a fundamental category of the way we experience our human existence. It is more than mere extension or distance. "Place" is interpreted space defined in relation to communities of people or to human significance more broadly. In other words, the meaning of place is humanly constructed. Place is "a complex network of relationships, connections and continuities ... of physical, social and cultural conditions that describe my actions, my responses, my awareness and that gives shape and content to the every life that is me."[4]

Any analysis of place inevitably has a subjective element. Our most common experience of place is our connection with familiar landscapes. We learn to discover who we are by relating to the landscapes of childhood or to adopted landscapes that become significant later because of particular associations. "Place" and historical memory, whether personal or collective, are closely associated. "Place is space which has historical meanings, where some things have happened which are now remembered and which provide continuity and identity across generations."[5] For any one with historical sensitivities such as me, there can be no more powerful experience than to visit or to live in a place with a vibrant sense of "continuities." Our presence, our present, in any given place is connected to a myriad other human presences in the past. Such a sense of place marks you for life. Landscapes are the geography of our imagination.

Badbury Rings, near where I lived as a child, is a tree-covered hill encircled by ancient earth ramparts. It is the reputed site of one of the great battles (Mons Badonicus) of the legendary King Arthur of Britain who supposedly defeated the invading Saxon hordes sometime in the late fifth century CE and kept the light of "civilization" and Christianity flickering for a few more years.[6] Legend has it that no bird will sing in the trees because of the great slaughter that took place there all those centuries ago. Collective memory materialized in landscape? Well, the silence of the place is certainly palpable.

Landscape in my native land is never pure. Not only is it shaped by enclosure or agriculture or forestation, it is also named. Names give the landscape a shape and a meaning in relation to human encounters. No name is arbitrary. Every name, even a single word, is a code that, if understood, unlocks a world of associations, events, people and their stories. Almost everywhere in my part of England there is a heavy layer of Anglo-Saxon. In some places there is a faint Celtic memory. There are a number of Roman hints and the occasional Norman reference. The small cathedral city where I presently work, Salisbury, is an excellent example. "Salisbury" is a Norman variant (substituting an "l" for an "r") of a Saxon name Searobyrg (derived from Searaburg) meaning "armor fort." But this in turn hints at the older Roman name Sorviodunum. The first element was treated by Saxons as a sound and transposed into their word for "armor." The second element, "dunum," was simply translated into the Saxon equivalent for "fort." But the Roman name itself has older resonances for it is really Romano-British and the second element is actually the Celtic word dunon.[7]

We cannot but be culturally conditioned in terms of the landscapes that exercise power over us. This can be detected in the distinctive approach to landscape painting in different countries. For example, those of us who live on the islands of Britain live in a relatively small country with very few "grand" landscapes (and changeable weather). In contrast, the American Rockies and plains are overwhelming in their vastness and the desert at the heart of Australia is disconcerting in its emptiness.[8] We tend to be struck by a combination of small natural features and the subtle play of light and shadow cast by clouds.

This British sense of the particular, the small and immediate in landscapes marks the way we perceive the sacred as well. I recall my several visits to the holy island of Iona off the West coast of Scotland where the great Irish saint, Columba, founded his center of monasticism in the sixth century CE. It was from there that Christianity spread across Scotland and the North of England. In terms of natural features, Iona is small and relatively insignificant compared to other Scottish islands. It is only about three-and-a half miles long by about one-and-a half miles wide, there are very few trees or plants and the highest point rises a mere 350 feet above sea level. As with all small islands on the northern edge of Europe, the weather on Iona is variable, frequently wild and unwelcoming. Yet, Iona has sometimes been described as a "thin place" where the membrane between the material world and the world of spiritual realities is particularly thin.

What gives Iona this special quality that attracts thousands of people from all over the world who come as pilgrims and tourists or those with an uncertainty as to what they are? The tangible "spirit of place" that appears to strike most visitors immediately is probably a mixture of a profound sense of a historically and spiritually significant place in the landscape, its barren wildness, the striking effects of light, and the beauty of smallness. With no majestic mountains in sight (unlike the next door island of Mull), one's eyes tend to be drawn downwards into the myriad rockpools on the shoreline to notice the extraordinary range of tone, color and shape of the small rocks and pebbles as they are washed by the sea.

It is worth remembering too that, for people of the British Isles, the natural feature above all others is the sea. This, more than anything else, has inspired English and various forms of Celtic art, music, poetry and a sense of the numinous. On a personal note, the seascape near my childhood home was infinitely varied, shaped and reshaped by the ever-changing effects of light, wind, sky and tides. The sea also had many voices – the deep roar of breakers or the whisper of water on shingled beaches. As a child, the sea spoke to me of an immense reality enfolding me that evoked awe, yet in which I could be at home. As I grew older and left home, I lost touch with the sea, with place, for several years, and this separation accentuated a sense of disconnection with my experience of the sacred and of self.

If we are placeless people without roots we are not only insecure but also in danger of abusing the world and people around us in a vain attempt to create an artificial identity we do not naturally experience. Cultural historians and social anthropologists agree that "place" is a universal human category (though not with a universal definition) without which human groups cannot exist because it is a fundamental framework for the human experience of relating to self, to other people and to the world. As the philosopher Martin Heidegger suggests, "Place is the house of being."[9]

Unfortunately, the meaning of places is frequently contested. They do not have a single, fundamental "meaning." Recent reflections on the subject tend to note the plurality of meanings given to particular places by those who relate to them. In my own islands, Northern Ireland is a case in point. Even the different ways the place is named – Ulster, Northern Ireland, the North of Ireland – express conflicting understandings of the history, ethnic identity and social structures of a place. As the title of a recent volume on pilgrimage, *Contesting the Sacred*, suggests, even sacred places are just as likely to cause divisions as provoke a consensus of interpretation. The classic example given is the city of Jerusalem in which no less than three world faiths contest the meaning of sacred sites.[10]

My central point is that the power of place stems predominantly from cultural factors or human associations. Whatever they are, our personal landscapes seem to evoke a profound sense of being rooted – not simply there in the specific place but also in ourselves, in life, in the *saeculum*, the here and now. Kathleen Norris in an essay on "spiritual geography" writes powerfully of "the place where I've wrestled my story out of the circumstances of landscape and inheritance."[11] At the same time, landscapes frequently have a capacity to carry us beyond ourselves and beyond the immediate. They are often our first intimations of the sacred.

Notes

1. Michel de Certeau, *The Mystic Fable*, vol 1, ET, University of Chicago Press, Chicago, 1992, p. 299.
2. See Anne Buttimer, "Home, Reach and the Sense of Place," in: Anne Buttimer and David Seamon, eds., *The Human Experience of Space and Place*, Croom Helm, London, 1980, p. 174.
3. Arnold Berleant, *The Aesthetics of Environment*, Temple University Press, Philadelphia, 1992, pp. 86-87.
4. Ibid p. 4. On the humanly constructed meaning of "place" see also Simon Schama, *Landscape and Memory*, HarperCollins, London, 1995, for example pp. 6-7, 61 and 81.
5. Walter Brueggemann, *The Land: Place as Gift, Promise and Challenge in Biblical Faith*, Fortress, Philadelphia, 1977, p. 5.
6. CE refers to the modern British designation for our dating system, "Common Era," in place of AD which specifically refers to "Anno Domini" or "the year of Our Lord [Jesus Christ]."
7. Martyn Whittock, *Wiltshire Place-Names: Their Origins and Meanings*. Countryside

Books, Newbury, 1997, p. 122 and Eilert Ekwall, *The Concise Oxford Dictionary of English Place-Names*, Clarendon Press, Oxford, 1985 edition, p. 402.

8. On the "spirituality" implied by landscape art see Peter Fuller, *Theoria: Art and The Absence of Grace*, London, 1988, especially Chapters 14 "An Earthly Paradise?," 19 "The Art of England," 21 "The Glare of the Antipodes."

9. Martin Heidegger, "Building dwelling thinking," in: *Poetry, Language, Thought*, Harper & Row, New York, 1975, pp. 145-61.

10. See John Eade & Michael Sallnow, eds., *Contesting the Sacred: The Anthropology of Christian Pilgrimage*, Routledge, London, 1990, Introduction, passim.

11. Kathleen Norris, *Dakota: A Spiritual Geography*, Houghton Mifflin, New York, 1993, p. 2.

John Carey

THE HEART OF KNOWING

How is the mind to live its life, in the coming time? I shall begin this sequence of reflections with the parable which Plato put near the end of his dialogue, *Phaedrus*. Socrates tells how, once upon a time, the Egyptian god Theuth – the inventor of mathematics and geometry and astronomy, of games of skill and chance, and of the art of writing – brought all of his discoveries to the divine king Thamus. He explained the merits of each, saying of writing that "this knowledge, O king, will render the Egyptians wiser and better able to remember; for it represents the discovery of a medicine for memory and wisdom." But his master saw the matter otherwise, replying,

> O you most ingenious of the gods! It is one man's task to bring an art into being; but it falls to another to judge what harm or benefit that art is destined to bestow upon those who will make use of it. And now you, being their father, have out of fondness assigned to letters the opposite of their (true) power.
>
> For this art will bring forgetfulness to the souls of those who learn it, through failure to exercise the memory: trusting in writing, they will make use of various external

signs, not of those forms which are within, in order to recollect. Indeed, it is not a medicine for memory, but a medicine for reminding which you have discovered.

You provide your students not with truth, but with an appearance of wisdom. For, becoming acquainted with many things while lacking instruction, they will seem to know much, but will in most respects be ignorant and unpleasant to live with; for they will have become wise in their own eyes, rather than truly so.[1]

Socrates goes on to draw the moral that living discourse is the only effective medium of thought.

Plato was a master of irony, and there are many ironies here. The fable which Socrates has related concerning the preciousness of oral tradition is, he claims, itself a tradition, a "thing heard": but his companion Phaedrus easily discerns that Socrates has made it up then and there. The greatest irony, however, is in Plato's own relationship to the story: for he has of course written Socrates's denunciation of writing. In doing so, he has underlined a paradox fundamental to all his dialogues: while maintaining that the search for truth is to be pursued in converzation, Plato himself created works of written literature, in which the spontaneity of speech is counterfeited by the static arrangement of letters on a page.

How are we to understand this contradiction? I do not think it adequate to suppose that Plato was simply *unaware* of it;[2] or that, turning a blind eye to the benefits which he had himself derived from literacy, he aspired to turn the clock back on behalf of others.[3] In fact he was, as is well known, harshly critical of the poetic culture of preliterate Greece, and it has been persuasively argued that his own achievement reflects the impact of writing's cultural ascendancy: "Plato, living in the midst of this revolution, announced it and became its prophet."[4]

I suggest that it is not writing versus orality *per se* with which Plato is concerned in the fable of Theuth, but rather the difference between the two modes of apprehension which he calls "memory" and "reminding" – between the possession of knowledge within our own minds, and a dependence on external repositories of information. Literacy does not of course *necessitate* the latter condition; but it makes it possible, and in many ways encourages it. Plato, while not seriously calling for the abandonment of writing, wishes nevertheless to warn us of this risk which it entails.

And why should it be seen as a risk? What, in the end, distinguishes "memory" from "reminding"? Nothing at all, presumably, if we are simply thinking machines, storing and manipulating data. But of course we are more than this. We are living intelligences, transformed by every idea which we take into ourselves, and transforming those ideas in their turn. There is all the difference in the world between information which we can "access," and that which has become a part of our own being: flavoring our speech, coloring our perceptions, lurking in our dreams. This is some of what A. K. Coomaraswamy had in mind when he stated that "from the Indian point of view a man can only be said to *know* what he knows *by heart*; what he must go to a book to be reminded of, he merely knows of."[5]

Let us look again at Thamus's concluding words: "You provide your students not with truth, but with an appearance of wisdom. For, becoming acquainted with many things while lacking instruction, they will seem to know much, but will in most respects be ignorant and unpleasant to live with; for they will have become wise in their own eyes, rather than truly so."

What divides wisdom from its empty semblance is the vital presence of the teacher: it is because they take knowledge in "without instruction" that those who trust entirely to reading are essentially ignorant. Again, the emphasis is on a personal encounter with knowledge, and on the inner awakening which can result from this. As Plato says of the pursuit of philosophy in his *Seventh Letter*:

> It is necessary to study [good and evil] at the same time that one studies the false and the true in the whole of existence, taking all pains and spending a long time at it ... When each of these things – names and statements, appearances and perceptions – was laboriously compared with the others, examined in friendly discussion, employing questions and answers without envy: then the intellect and

mind of each, straining human capacity to the utmost possible, were filled with light.

No one seriously concerned with such matters would attempt to replace this process with a written account: such a text, falling into the hands of the uninitiated, would produce only "envy and consternation."[6]

The highest mode of learning is not the accumulation of facts, but the mind's training for enlightenment. And such enlightenment is, for Plato, the truest kind of memory: a recollection of what the soul knew before birth, and still preserves hidden within itself.[7]

We can compare all of this with an anecdote from China, a generation or two after Plato's time. The Taoist sage Chuang Tzu relates how a humble wheelwright told Duke Hwan, as the latter sat on a dais reading "the words of the sages," that he was only busying himself with "the dregs and sediments of those old men."

> The duke said, "How should you, a wheelwright, have anything to say about the book which I am reading? If you can explain yourself, very well; if you cannot, you shall die!" The wheelwright said, "Your servant will look at the thing from the point of view of his own art. In making a wheel, if I proceed gently, that is pleasant enough, but the workmanship is not strong; if I proceed violently, that is toilsome and the joinings do not fit. If the movements of my hand are neither (too) gentle nor (too) violent, the idea in my mind is realized. But I cannot tell (how to do this) by word of mouth; there is a knack to it. I cannot teach the knack to my son, nor can my son learn it from me.... But these ancients, and what it was not possible for them to convey, are dead and gone: so then what you, my Ruler, are reading is but their dregs and sediments!"[8]

These words too are not without their irony, as we read them more than two millennia later! What can their relevance be to us? And has the passage which I have cited from Plato's *Seventh Letter* anything to say to our culture as a whole, or does it only describe the experience of philosophers and mystics?

We have seen both Plato and Chuang Tzu speak of a kind of knowledge which is an integral part of the knower. When such knowledge can be communicated at all, this communication is a mystery or miracle. It flames forth like a spark within the mind, transforming the awareness: and the awareness must already have been strenuously disciplined before the spark can be attained. Such epiphanies are milestones in the search for wisdom, for holiness, for beauty, for justice, and for any of the forms of truth.

But even if we do not feel ready to attempt the heights, we can recognize that *any* knowledge, if it is to change or ennoble us, if it is to help us toward the completion of our being, must be taken fully into ourselves. Plato, who saw writing as a system of external signs, as a *substitute* for inner knowledge, feared that it would prevent this intimate assimilation. The reader would absorb the words, but not the living teaching of which those words had been the vehicle: he would be left with nothing but "dregs and sediments."

Happily, the unfolding of literate civilization has not realized all of Plato's fears. Experience has shown that we can in fact turn what we read into an essential component of ourselves. Indeed, writing makes possible a privacy and individuality of expression which invite the thoughtful reader to enter minds remote in time and space. A poet of the Middle Ages gives us a beautiful example of this, in a verse for a tombstone:

> Do you wish to know, traveller, whether
> poets live after death?
> Behold: what you read, I utter. Truly,
> your voice is my own.[9]

But to say that what Plato feared has not come to pass is not to say that he had nothing to be afraid of. The alphabet, and the printing press which so radically amplified the alphabet's effect, have in the event not divided us from the ability to transform ourselves through learning. But does that mean that nothing can so divide us?

A computer can "remember" incomparably more than can be stored in any human brain; given the right instructions, it can sift this ocean of data at dizzying speed, retrieving just those items which its operator requires. Now, moreover, any single machine can tap into a seemingly limitless network beyond itself, a labyrinth of interwoven conduits of information. The new technology can, far more than mere writing, accomplish everything of which Theuth boasted. But it also represents, far more than writing, the dangers of which Thamus warned.[10]

It is not my concern to find fault with such technical imperfections as may exist within this system, or with the trivial or destructive uses to which it can be put. This would be beside the point, and in any case a waste of ink or breath: the computer is here to stay, and its development represents a triumph of human inventiveness. It would be foolish not to recognize this achievement, and doubly foolish not to acknowledge the extraordinary power of the tool which has been placed in our hands.

But what if the tool begins to master the user? We can consider a commonplace example. Let us say that a scholar is studying the *Upanishads*, and wishes to compare all of the instances of a certain collocation of words. Unless he has memorized the material in its entirety – and for the purposes of our illustration we can discount this increasingly improbable scenario – even the simplest project of this kind would until recently have involved the reading (even if this were only skimming) of hundreds of pages of text. But now, if the *Upanishads* are on a disk and the scholar issues the correct command, his computer can find what he wants within seconds. He may not even need to have typed the material into it in the first place: a good enough scanner (and here too the technology is constantly improving) could do the lion's share of this work for him.

Hours or days or weeks of toil have been saved – so far as this goes, it is admirable, and opens up exhilarating vistas and opportunities. But perceive the cost. In carrying out his task, apart from striking some keys and then reading off the result, our scholar has entered into no direct contact with what he is studying: it remains *outside* him. We are on our way from a conception of knowledge as a part of the living fabric of culture, a means of enriching our individual and collective being, to the view that it is a vast inorganic Other which only a computer, or a network of computers, can contain. The scholar, in such a scheme of things, is no omniscient emperor of data: he is more like a worker in some enormous factory, tending a machine of which he is now merely an extension.[11]

Information technology has, I believe, brought us closer than we have ever come before to the state of ignorance and forgetfulness of which Thamus spoke: a world in which machines will do our knowing for us, and our own minds will be empty of whatever is not being projected there by an exterior stimulus.[12] It is not enough that pressing a button can bring everything back (even if that were true): what is not within us does not really belong to us. It is a kind of knowledge which cannot turn into wisdom.[13]

But it is not the computer, or any other modern contrivance, which is to blame in this: otherwise Plato could not have foreseen our danger two and a half thousand years ago. The responsibility lies with ourselves,[14] and with underlying attitudes whose seeds he could even then discern.

The computer was developed, in the first instance, to confront the challenge of *quantity*: a volume of information, originally (and still essentially) numerical, whose bulk could not be encompassed by merely human faculties. It is precisely this challenge which, millennia earlier, occasioned the invention of writing. Lewis Mumford makes this point in a discussion of the "megamachines," vast orchestrations of specialized human labor, which accomplished the monumental feats of antiquity:

> The written word ... went along historically with the control of large numbers; and it is no accident that the earliest uses of writing were not to convey ideas, religious or otherwise, but to keep temple records of grain, cattle, pottery, fabricated goods, stored and disbursed. This happened early, for a pre-dynastic Narmer mace in the Ashmolean Museum at Oxford records the taking of 120,000 prisoners, 400,000 oxen, and 1,422,000 goats. The arithmetical reckoning was an even greater feat than the capture.[15]

Even if it were possible, it would be absurd to commit information of this kind to memory. And as societies grow larger and more complex, there is more and more such information to be dealt with – external supplements to memory come into being to meet this need. With this I can see nothing wrong. The danger is in being overawed by bigness and speed, by the swelling mountains of data and the ever more powerful technologies with which we seek to master them – in coming to believe that we grow in knowledge insofar as we become more able to encounter this flood of facts *on its own level.* In Simone Weil's words, "The spirit, overcome by the weight of quantity, has no longer any other criterion than efficiency."[16]

To the extent that we succumb to this seduction, our minds will become components of the "megamachine" in its contemporary incarnation. It is intriguing to see Soren Kierkegaard, long before the computer age, recognizing not only the soullessness of such knowledge but also (like Mumford and Plato) its foreshadowings in ancient Egypt:

> The law for the development of the self with respect to knowing, insofar as it is the case that the self becomes itself, is that the increase of knowledge corresponds to the increase of self-knowledge, that the more the self knows, the more it knows itself. If this does not happen, the more knowledge increases, the more it becomes a kind of inhuman knowledge, in the obtaining of which a person's self is squandered, much the way men were squandered on building pyramids.[17]

Such slavery, like all slavery, can end by persuading us that it is our true nature. We can forget that knowledge is ever more than a quantifiable commodity, external to ourselves; and if we acquiesce to such estrangement, our relationship with what we know will degenerate into one of sterile exploitation. Some of the intellectual consequences of so acquiescing are suggested in two further passages: one from a lecture delivered by Friedrich Schiller in 1789, the other from a piece written two centuries later by Wendell Berry.

Schiller is contrasting the academic hireling, whom he calls the "bread-scholar" (*brotgelehrte*), with the "philosophic mind":

> The former, whose diligence has as its one and only goal fulfilling the conditions which will qualify him for his job, and enable him to enjoy its privileges ... will when he

embarks on his academic training have no higher concern than that of scrupulously separating those subjects which he names "bread-studies" from those which satisfy the spirit as spirit only. All the time which he devoted to the latter has been, he believes, stolen from his future profession: and for this theft he will never forgive himself.... He does not seek a reward in the treasures of his mind – he expects it from the recognition of others, from prestigious posts, from affluence. If these things elude him, who is more unfortunate than the bread-scholar? In vain has he lived, remained wakeful, toiled. He has sought for truth in vain, if truth cannot be transformed for him into gold, the praise of newspapers, the favor of princes....

How different is the approach of the philosophic mind! All his strivings are devoted to the completion of his knowledge. His noble impatience cannot rest until all of his ideas have arranged themselves in a harmonious whole – until he stands in the midst of his art, of his discipline, and from there surveys its expanse with a contented gaze.[18]

Berry refers to these two types as the "professional" and the "amateur," remembering in the case of the latter word its original meaning "lover":[19]

Professional standards, the standards of ambition and selfishness, are always sliding downward toward expense, ostentation, and mediocrity. They tend always to narrow the ground of judgment. But amateur standards, the standards of love, are always striving upward toward the humble and the best. They enlarge the ground of judgment. The context of love is the world.[20]

How is the mind to live its life, in the coming time?

Answers can be sought, and much achieved, in writing, in lecturing, in attempts to reform educational systems. But the final answer must lie, as it has always done, in each of us individually. We must each learn to recognize a distinction between two kinds of knowledge: one pertaining to the outer world, and the incalculable multiplicity of its disparate phenomena; the other forming a part of an internal journey, and participating in the wholeness of our being. The essential difference, as Blake never tired of saying, is not in what is known but in how it is known. If we do at last come to the place of illumination, we will not need to write down what we find there: as Plato knew, "there is no risk that anyone would forget that, if once he should clasp it with his soul; for it abides in the shortest [formulations] of all."[21]

The key to such knowing – whose other name is wisdom – is the love of what one seeks to know: the philosophic love of the amateur. As an image for such intellectual love, we can meditate on one of the turning-points of the Christian revelation: the miracle of Pentecost. From throughout the world, the speakers of innumerable languages have gathered together in the city. But it is those to whom the Spirit has come like fire who can speak to the multitudes in a single voice.[22]

Notes

1. *Phaedrus*, 274e-275b; my translation.
2. Eric A. Havelock, *Preface to Plato* (Cambridge, Massachusetts, 1963), 56 n. 16, describes Plato's position here as "not only conservative but illogical"; for Walter J. Ong, *Orality and Literacy: The Technologizing of the Word* (London, 1982), 80-1, "Plato of course was not at all fully aware of the unconscious forces at work in his psyche to produce this reaction, or overreaction, of the literate person to lingering, retardant orality." The fable's "inconsistency" is more appreciatively considered in Jacques Derrida's essay "Plato's pharmacy," in *Dissemination*, trans. Barbara Johnson (Chicago, 1981), 61-171: an ingeniously nuanced treatment, whose premises however differ fundamentally from those of the present discussion.
3. E. G. Turner, cited in Havelock, loc. cit., speaks of Plato as fighting "a rearguard action" in this passage.
4. Havelock, *Preface to Plato*, i. This seminal book presents a valuable analysis of many aspects of the question being considered here. Much of Havelock's argument is summarized on page 189: "It may indeed be suggested that it was increasing alphabetization which opened the way to experiments in abstraction. Once rid of the need to preserve experience vividly, the composer was freer to reorganize it reflectively."
5. A. K. Coomaraswamy, *The Bugbear of Literacy* (London, 1949), 32.
6. *Seventh Letter*, 344b-c; my translation.
7. See the illuminating discussion by A. K. Coomaraswamy, "Recollection, Indian and Platonic," in *Coomaraswamy*, ed. Roger Lipsey, 3 vols (Princeton, 1977), ii.49-65.
8. Chuang Tzu, XIII.10, in *The Texts of Taoism*, trans. James Legge, 2 vols (Oxford, 1891; repr. New York, 1962), i.343-4.
9. My translation; the original reads "*Viuere post mortem uates uis nosse uiator?/Quod legis*

ecce loquor, uox tua nempe mea est." I have mislaid (forgotten!) the source of this verse.

10. This analogy with Plato's observations (or rather this extension of them) has been noted among others by Iris Murdoch, *Metaphysics as a Guide to Morals* (London, 1993), 18-19.

11. In itself, the quest for truth in matters of minute detail is an essential service to humanity: what I find disquieting in the mechanistic research considered here is not its *humbleness* but its *alienation*. Compare Simone Weil, *Gravity and Grace*, trans. Emma Craufurd (London, 1963), 139: "As collective thought cannot exist as thought, it passes into things (signs, machines ...). Hence the paradox: it is the thing which thinks and the man who is reduced to the status of a thing."

12. Cf. Murdoch, *Metaphysics as a Guide to Morals*, 210: "We are (in ways both fortunate and unfortunate) destined to become surrounded by, used to, dependent on, clever machines which separate us from the old simpler furniture of the world and even from the activity of our own minds.... What is, and not implausibly, envisaged here is an apocalyptic change in human consciousness, involving vast social changes and the disappearance of old local ideas of individuals and virtues. A loss of sovereignty." She adds (and the same point should be stressed regarding the present essay) that this forecast is not a prophecy, but rather an extrapolation from current trends: "We cannot see the future, but must fear it intelligently" (211).

13. This point must be insisted on, despite the intoxicating possibilities made available by the new technology (most notably the Internet). That enhanced access to knowledge does not *as such* lead to self-transformation is perhaps most evident, ironically enough, in the words of the enthusiasts who believe that they have found a "spiritual," "transcendent" plane of being in "cyberspace." Illustrations of the impoverishment of these conceptions may be found in the seventh chapter of Margaret Wertheim's book *The Pearly Gates of Cyberspace: A History of Space from Dante to the Internet* (London, 1999): an account rendered all the more damning by the author's evenhanded approach to her material.

14. This is already implicit in Plato's contrast between "memory" and "reminding," both mental processes. Derrida comments that "the boundary (between inside and outside, living and nonliving) separates not only speech from writing but also memory as an unveiling (re-)producing a presence from re-memoration as the mere repetition of a monument; truth as distinct from its sign, being as distinct from types" (*Dissemination*, 108-9).

15. Lewis Mumford, *The Myth of the Machine: Technics and Human Development* (New York, 1966), 192; Narmer was an Egyptian king who flourished c. 2900 BC. More recent findings, corroborating the evidence known to Mumford, are cited by J. Ong, *Orality and Literacy*, 86. Mumford characterizes the "megamachine" itself as "an invisible structure composed of living, but rigid, human parts, each assigned to his special office, role, and task, to make possible the immense work-output and grand designs of this great collective organization" (189).

16. Simone Weil, *Gravity and Grace*, 140. Compare page 84: "A number which increases thinks that it is getting near to infinity. It is receding from it."

17. S. Kierkegaard, *The Sickness unto Death*, trans. H. V. Hong and E. H. Hong (Princeton, 1981), 31.

18. From "Was heißt und zu welchem Ende studiert man Universalgeschichte?," in *Schillers Werke*, ed. Gerhard Stenzel, 2 vols (Salzburg, n.d.), ii.684-6; my translation.

19. Schiller too, in speaking of the "philosophic" mind, uses a word which originally designated the *love* of wisdom.

20. Wendell Berry, *What Are People For?* (San Francisco, 1990), 90. Compare Weil, *Gravity and Grace*, 56-7: "The mind is not forced to believe in the existence of anything.... That is why the only organ of contact with existence is acceptance, love. That is why beauty and reality are identical. That is why joy and the sense of reality are identical."

21. *Seventh Letter*, 344c; my translation.

22. Acts of the Apostles 2:1-11. Writing in the ninth century, Anastasius the Librarian said of the scholar Eriugena that the Holy Spirit had made him "both burning and eloquent ... for love was his school-mistress" (cited in my article "Symbol and mystery in Irish religious thought," *Temenos* 13 (1992) 101-11: 105).

Ranjit Hoskote

BEACONS OF SAINTHOOD

The saint is the archetypal figure of faith. As the embodiment of a moral imagination it is one that enriches itself and others through its engagement with the cycles of suffering and doubt. In a world tormented by demons of its own making, the saint also represents the possibility that compassion and illumination can be recovered from the acid flow of history. By some law of culture, however, all objects of veneration gradually suffer a transformation into objects of denigration, and the saint, sooner or later becomes the target of scorn. The aura of the saint is sought to be sullied in more cynical periods precisely because he or she comes to represent an impossible ideal of perfection in thought and conduct: an ideal so remote from us in its perfection that our vulnerabilities are exposed by contrast, to our discomfiture and eventual rage.

It is this sense of having been robbed of personal capability by a superhuman exemplar, perhaps, that once led a critic of the religious life to say to me, with some asperity, that the world stands in no real need of saints. He was particularly annoyed with the tendency to confer a contemporary relevance on the guides and prophets of tradition, rendering them acceptable for secular consumption as proto-scientists, proto-feminists or proto-environmentalists. In that a person's (even a saint's) contribution – to physics, music, the liberation of women from patriarchal norms or the conservation of the environment – stems from material human effort, ran my interlocutor's argument, it has nothing to do with the Divine, or with a transcendent dimension of experience. In other words, in this view, we can get on with discovering subatomic particles, protesting outrages against women or saving the rain forests as rational human beings, without contriving to summon Milarepa, Mira, Schweitzer or St. Francis to our aid.

This line of argument suggests that a saint's pursuits cannot possibly concern humanity at large except as a curiosity, since he or she is essentially concerned with an individual quest for communion with the Divine, an incommunicable experience of bliss. That is to say, a saint's religious preoccupations are too private to be relevant in social terms, while his or her social preoccupations can be arrived at by others without reference to religion. While such an argument can devalue and trivialize even the most precious resources of hope, it must nevertheless be treated seriously by everyone – orthodox believer and secular activist alike – then invoke the values and deeds of the saints, Sufis or *siddhas* for contemporary purposes. Its polemical scepticism exposes a selectiveness in our reading of religion: while believers enshrine the saint as a mystic given to occasional bursts of revolution, activists extol him or her as a social revolutionary slowed down by some embarrassing mystical baggage. In this separation of the two aspects of every saint's personality lies the considerable danger of misrepresentation and distortion. A religious genius bears the values of transformation at many, sometimes irreconcilable levels, and the mystic cannot be isolated from the revolutionary: both aspects are crucially important to an understanding of sainthood.

How, then, are holiness and radicalism to be understood in the uneasy but richly dynamic relation in which they stand to each other? When we speak of St. Francis of Assisi, do we mean the rich merchant's son who silenced his vanity, mortifying it by kissing lepers' sores, or do we mean the spirited protector of animals and birds, who discoursed with the man-eating wolf; and how did the two aspects impinge upon each other? How do we treat Mira's choice of Krishna-bhakti: do we praise it as an escape from, and a rebellion against, the stifling bondage of feudal patriarchy; or do we deplore it as an act of abject self-surrender before the Divine bodied forth in Krishna? Do we cherish Kabir as the serene celebrant of the Holy Name, or as the weaver who attacked the dogmas of the established order? The same dilemma has faced us, nearer in time, in the matter of Mother Teresa. Is she to be remembered as the orthodox Catholic who denounced abortion as an act of murder, and who was accused of cultivating poverty and suffering as states conducive to the love of God? Or shall we, instead, treasure the woman who, more than any of her liberal or socialist critics, dedicated herself to the service of the dying and the destitute?

The truth is that saints are complex and often self-contradictory individuals; it is a mistake to straitjacket them as perfect machines of righteousness, consistent within themselves and executing a coherent ideological programme. It often happens that one component of a saint's work achieves universal significance, while another remains imprisoned within its time horizon. In the same personality, radical creative insight may exist beside unquestioning conformity with dead tradition. Saints inhabit an extremely dangerous spiritual minefield. They may become trapped by the routine performance of good acts, by the expectations of the devout. Sometimes, also, history overtakes the saints: the emancipatory language of divine love fades away, leaving behind only the cadences of subjection, as with Chaitanya and Mira, whose revolt against the repressive orthodoxy was phrased in the language of uninhibited love-surrender to the Lord, an idiom then viable but now suspect. Or then the sacred teachings may become available without necessarily involving the prerequisite of faith: we may emulate the saint's love for created beings without particularly desiring communion with the Creator. At the risk of sounding flippant, for instance, we may observe that the Bodhisattvas' striking initiatives of compassion, demonstrated in a world dominated by sacred consciousness, are now replicated at a less ambitious degree by pressure groups like Greenpeace or altruistic institutions like the SPCA.

And yet we cannot seem to exist without saints: if none are available, we invent them. Some of us cling to the *Bhaktavali*, the *Dasacharita* or the *Tadqirat-i-Auliya*. Or else, having lost contact with these traditional storehouses of wisdom, we hold on to the newspapers and the television screen. Before our eyes, a princess who led a life of tragic, confused and largely hedonistic impulses becomes transmuted into an icon of compassion. If the transfiguration of Princess Diana can safely be dismissed as a case of canonization by television, millions of people in India turn, in their distress, to such genuine bearers of hope and resilience as the Dalai Lama, Baba Amte, Anna Hazare, Chandi Prasad Bhatt, Sunderlal Bahuguna and Medha Patkar, as they have in the past to Mahatma Gandhi, Schweitzer and other exemplars of asceticism, courage and compassion.

What is it that prompts us to return to the martyrs, teachers and sages, beyond an anthropological interest in the collection of legends? Is it, perhaps, the need to make contact with figures who have incarnated our confusions and vulnerabilities, but have found a way out of the circle of fire? In modern times, as in ancient or medieval ones, we reinterpret these radiant and universal figures in ways that seem to address or even answer our own specific crises. There is, however, a crucial difference between the ancient or medieval sensibility and ours in this matter: it is the difference between hagiography and criticism. Our ancestor's belief in the emulation of the lives of saints was focused on the latter's ultimate resolution of their crises; they lived in a framework of consciousness that admitted the security of ultimate goals. We, on the other hand, live in an age of deferred resolutions and shattered teleologies; consequently, in attending to the lives of the saints, we tend to be far more interested in the struggle leading up to the resolution. While the saints' resolution of their crises served as a hagiographic standard by which ordinary morality could theoretically be judged in earlier times, the present obliges us to be less concerned with the resolution and more critically preoccupied with the textures of their conflicts, dilemmas and strategies along the way.

If we are unsure of how the saint is to be regarded today, this is because we are mentally divided between the earlier hagiographic attitude and the current critical one. In the circumstances, our critical attitude leads us to render the saints the highest possible praise by reenacting their passion, emulating their courage and concern, testing their example and precept by translating these directly into action. The other, less demanding but more popular attitude leads us to worship the saints for their attainment of an enlightened or perfected state, without attempting to learn adaptively from these precedents. This is scarcely useful, for it prompts us to treat the saints as abstract persons, not as actors in history or in particular histories. Only when we see the saints in their existential context can we form a determinate connection between our intention and their example. Hemmed in by obstacles and temptations though they were, the saints in every culture have held fast to their aim, which is that of extending the human personality in terms of love, faith, hope, creativity, compassion, and so trying to overcome the limitations placed on the questing self by the prevailing moral environment. The bridging of the gap between intention and example defines the bridging of the distance between what we are and what we hope to become – it constitutes the wager that we place on transcendence.

It is when we mistake the wager for a guarantee that we become trapped in a misunderstanding about the saint's perfection. The simple truth is that the saint is not perfect (certainly not in the neurotic and absolutist sense in which we understand perfection today). Perhaps we project such an idea of perfection on the saint in order to compensate for our own manifest imperfections: we make him or her the scapegoat for our lapses and inadequacies. But the saint is heir to error, as we all are; error is the visible form of our human limitations, the evidence that turns our consciousness in the direction of improvement, if not of perfectibility. What distinguishes the saint from the rest of us is that, with him or her, error does not remain a habit but becomes a door to discovery. Error, for the saint, leads to the discovery of the self's potentialities of renewal and refinement, that ever-thwarted but never abandoned hope of self-transformation which invests the quest with its significance and positive meaning.

Few saints have been free of curious, sometimes bizarre and

even potentially alienating traits of behavior. Some have appeared to be quite mad, others contrary and cussed, quixotic in the conduct of family life and in their understanding of the realities of self-preservation in a hostile economy – Milarepa, Luipa and Tukaram come to mind. But this eccentricity is merely a symptom of the condition that sets them apart from other human beings, not the condition itself. What makes the saints different is the fact that they never lose sight of the higher objective of self-overcoming: their lives dramatize the shift, potentially available to all human beings through effort, from the realm of necessity to the realm of freedom.

To restrict the saint to a private relationship with God, then, is to reduce the wide span of associations that the saint can and does enact with society (and saints, as Camus observes, can be had without God too). The saint's real hazards are these: How to serve the creatures of the world with composure, while accepting the inability of humankind to explain the world's factuality, the mystery of our being in it? How to reconcile the end of liberating the world from horror and inequity, without being overtaken by the means of change? Such are the paradoxes of redemption that the saviors of the oppressed may grow to be as coarse and violent as the oppressors they fight, establishing structures that begin with a charter of emancipation but end as prisons more stifling than those they were meant to break down. This is the nature of the Utopian project of salvation in a secular frame, when institutional change is believed to be efficacious enough to bring about inner change, without spiritual discipline.

But the saint shows a sensitivity that is the opposite of Utopian absolutism, of that demonic propensity which (Kierkegaard observes), seeks the absolute in a world of relativities. By contrast, the saint is often actuated by an Arcadian belief in individual transformation within a loose community, and is alive to the vulnerability of humankind. It might be argued that many saints have oscillated between Utopia and Arcadia, or, in Weberian terms, between the revolutionary ethic, which commits its bearer to responsibility towards an ideal, and the mystical ethic, which commits its bearer to a love for others. At the point of greatest tension, though, they have dedicated themselves to the task of reconciling the two ethics into a unity of concern. This, too, is an approach to perfection – a wager, a cry sometimes voiced before the temple but more often voiced in the streets, under the banners of protest, without benefit of the Divine presence. Fittingly, it was Ignazio Silone, a co-founder of the Italian Communist Party, who best characterized the saint's quest (in *The Story of a Humble Christian*) as one predicated upon an "ever-disappointed, but tenacious hope."

It is not perfection, therefore, but the tenacious striving after perfection that makes the saint a saint. Hamstrung though he or she may be by historical adversities or self-created flaws, the saint remains committed to the goal of extending human potentiality. Hobbled by the negative emotions, the saint nevertheless aspires to achieve the natural, unforced practice of compassion, charity, faith. If we return to the saints, it is not because we see in them a grandiose image of what we could never be, but because we find in them compelling testimony to a life of self-experiment and self-discovery – this is an enabling, and not a disabling gesture. In this lies the continuing relevance of the saint.

John Haldane

WITH GOOD REASON

For most of the last two thousand years, philosophy and religion have co-existed fairly happily together. Indeed a number of the greatest philosophers in the Western tradition have also been theologically minded. The list includes the following: Augustine, Avicenna, Anselm, Maimonides, Aquinas, Bonaventure, Descartes, Spinoza, Leibniz, Locke, Berkeley, Kant, Reid, Hegel, and Kierkegaard. Yet today only a small minority of leading philosophers believe in God. I shall try to say why that is so and assess whether the current situation indicates that faith is contrary to reason.

Before that, however, I need to say why belief was previously more widespread among philosophers. One might suppose that the answer is a general cultural one. In the past people were more disposed to belief than they are today; philosophers share the general outlook of their times; hence it is to be expected that in more religious times, more of them will have been religious. Setting aside the question of whether philosophers do, in fact, share the beliefs of their cultures and times, the answer given is somewhat regressive. For it invites the further question of why in the past people in general were more disposed to religious belief than is the case today.

The change is due, principally, I think, to the impact of natural science and the ways of thinking to which it has given rise. About twenty years after the crucifixion, St. Paul wrote his Letter to the Romans in which we read the following:

> What can be known about God is plain to men for God has shown it to them. Ever since the creation of the world his invisible nature, namely his eternal power and deity, has been clearly perceived in the things that have been made (Romans 1:19-20).

Paul is not so much offering a proof here as reminding his readers of something they already accept. However, reasoning to the existence of God based on the wonder of nature was common in antiquity and would have been known to Paul and to educated Romans, Jews and converts. For example, in his dialogue *On the Nature of the Gods (De natura deorum)* composed around 45 BC but set some thirty years earlier, Cicero has the Stoic philosopher Quintus Lucillus Balbus speak as follows:

> The point seems scarcely to need affirming. What can be so obvious and clear, as we gaze up at the sky and observe the heavenly bodies, as that there is some divine power of surpassing intelligence by which they are ordered?
> (*The Nature of the Gods*, trans. P. G. Walsh, Oxford: Clarendon, 1997, Bk. 2, 4.)

In the centuries that followed, Jewish, Christian and Islamic thinkers developed a number of arguments designed to prove the existence of God. The ambition was to start with claims that are evident to any thoughtful person and to show that these entail (in the sense, logically imply) the existence of a creator. The most famous presentation of such arguments is to be found in the first part (*Prime pars*) of Aquinas's *Summa Theologiae* where St. Thomas sets out the five ways (*quinque viae*). My impression is that while many educated people, including philosophy and theology graduates, recognize the phrase "the five ways," very few have actually read the text. This is probably because it is expected that the proofs are forbiddingly difficult to understand or that they expressed these at great length and in strange language.

In fact, the arguments are presented in the course of a couple of pages; and in a translation that glosses technical terms they are not very hard to comprehend. Here, for example, are extracts from Aquinas's first and fifth ways as translated in recent times by Timothy McDermott.

> The first and most obvious way is based on change. We see things changing. Now anything changing is being changed by something else ... This something else, if itself changing, is being changed by yet another thing; and this last by another. Now we must stop somewhere, otherwise there will be no first cause of the change, and, as a result, no subsequent causes ... We arrive then at some first cause of change not itself being changed by anything, and this is what everybody understands by *God* ...
>
> The fifth way is based on the guidedness of nature. Goal-directed behavior is observed in all bodies obeying natural laws, even when they lack awareness. Their behavior hardly ever varies and the practical turns out well ... but nothing lacking awareness can tend to a goal except through direction by someone with awareness and understanding ... everything in nature, therefore, is directed to its goal by someone with understanding, and this we call *God*.
>
> (*St. Thomas Aquinas Summa Theologiae: A Concise Translation,* ed. T. McDermott, London: Methuen, 1989, pp. 12-4.)

Very broadly speaking, arguments from the world to God come in two forms. First, those which reason from the existence of something that might not have been to the existence of something that is necessary – these are grouped under the heading *cosmological arguments*. Second, those which reason from the orderly character of things to the existence of a designer – these are classified as *teleological arguments*. In crude forms, arguments of both sorts can be found in antiquity, and they became popular in the middle ages when they were carefully refined. They continued to be favored by philosophers through until the eighteenth century. Thereafter, however, they came to be questioned, and today they are highly contested.

There are several reasons for this decline in standing but I shall mention only two. The first is that in the medieval and early modern periods these arguments were very ambitiously presented as deductive demonstrations. That is to say, it was held that their premises were entirely evident and hence beyond doubt, and that the inference from these to the conclusion that God exists was unquestionable. The general effect of scepticism, developed in modern philosophy and largely maintained ever since, has been to cause philosophers and others to dispute whether any statement is beyond doubt or contention. Also, it has come to be held that there could be other explanations of the phenomena cited (whether we know what these explanations might be is another matter) and hence the very most that could be said is that these phenomena are more likely to have been produced by God than to have arisen naturally.

Consider, for example standard forms of (A) cosmological and (B) teleologial arguments:

A. 1. Some things change.
   2. If any thing changes then there must be an uncaused cause of change.
   3. Therefore there is an uncaused cause of change.

and

B. 1. Some things exhibit regularity.
   2. If any thing exhibits regularity then there must be an uncreated designer.
   3. Therefore there is an uncreated designer.

It might be thought that the first premise in each argument is indeed beyond dispute, but that fails to take account of the ingenuity of scepticism and other philosophical querying of the apparently evident. More significantly the second premise in each case is nowadays quite widely challenged. This is due, I suggest, to the influence of scientific thought.

To begin with the second argument, whereas it was once thought to be the case that the regularity of the tides, seasons, planetary motions, and so on, and the existence and operation of organs that benefit the animals that possess them, could only be explained by reference to an extra-natural source of order, these assumptions are now taken to be disproved by theoretical physics and Darwinian evolutionary theory. This is not the occasion to pursue these matters in detail but let me offer a couple of comments in defence of the theological proofs (I explore these issues at much greater length in my half of J. J. C. Smart and J. J. Haldane, *Atheism and Theism*, "Great Debates in Philosophy," Blackwell, Oxford, 1997).

The regularity evident in the universe from the macroscopic to the microscopic levels is well-attested. Even quantum phenomena exhibit significant statistical patterns. Although it may not be determinate when a microphysical particle will be emitted, the fact that this remains within a range of probability renders the effects systematic. So, whether we are dealing with determinate or probabilistic propensities, we still find nature to be orderly, and this is not self-explanatory. It may be said that were it not orderly, there would have been a cosmic collapse and certainly we would not have existed to raise our questions. If this is so, it hardly eliminates the wonder. Our existence allows the fact of natural order to be observed, but had we not existed that order would remain. The issue of the origin of order remains a real one. Either we look for an explanation or we say in advance that there is none to be found. Adopting the first option, it is hard to see what the conclusion could be save that order results from the activity of a creator. Adopting the second involves a markedly unscientific assumption. It ill-suits the scientifically minded, therefore, to say that belief in a creator is incompatible with the scientific outlook.

The Darwinian challenge to natural theology is more limited in scope, but it has been much more extensive in effect. Unlike the previous notion it does not (at least in Darwin's own version) challenge the claim that there is regularity, but only questions the suggestion that the utility of organic features calls for a divine explanation. Instead, it postulates random mutation among species groups, plus natural selection in virtue of the adaptive utility of mutant features given current environments. Thus, if some populations sprout hair and this offers protection against heat or cold then, *ceteris paribus*, these animals are more likely to survive and breed, and this or related features among their descendent groups will again be selected for survival. On it goes and by stages emerge highly adapted animals such as ourselves. Wonderful to contemplate and not difficult to explain.

So it is assumed. In fact, however, evolutionary explanations are far from compelling. First, there are features whose adaptive utility is difficult to demonstrate – such as consciousness, an aptitude for philosophy, theology and other abstract thought; and second, and more theoretically problematic, is the fact that the very process of evolution seems to require non-evolved features, principally the power of reproduction. No one supposes that one species evolves from another by a single step. Rather, the idea is that there is "cumulative selection": progressive sifting and sorting as the product of one phase of selection is subjected to another environmental test. This supposes that there is already in place some form of reproduction possessed by the original and successor generations. Yet it is an adaptive feature to be explained by selection no less than others. But how can it be? Selection operates over generations and successive generations only come into being through the replicative powers of their ancestors. These powers cannot themselves be the product of cumulative selection and so their existence remains to be explained. Contemporary science offers no explanation; but theism can and does in terms of God bestowing reproductive powers on parts of his creation.

Nothing said above is hostile to science. The point is only that while science is good at giving explanations of events and circumstances within nature, it is not equipped to explain the preconditions of the possibility of there being a natural order or of its containing reproductive organisms. The implication is not that science should be rejected but that the attempt to reject rational faith on the basis of purported "scientific world view" is bogus. I am claiming therefore, that there is life in the old arguments for the existence of God and that believers should equip themselves to defend their faith on the basis of reasoning that has the power to elicit respect from the genuinely scientifically minded.

What then, and finally, of faith itself? There is a style of argument, much favored in the last century and in the first half of this, that seeks to explain belief away by showing – or claiming to show – that it is the effect of certain natural causes. Examples of this tendency are theories in sociology that religion exists to serve certain social functions, in psychology that belief is the effect of infantile formation and a means of psychological defence against the fact of death, and in economics that it is one of the tools by which a privileged minority keeps in check an exploited majority. Such diagnoses are open to two objections. First, there is the question of their plausibility as explanations. When one looks hard at the facts of religious belief and practice, it is hard to credit them. Those who believe in God often give reasons that have weight quite independently of the believers' social, psychological and economic circumstances. There is not even any interesting correlation between faith and believers' social, psychological and economic situations.

Second, even if there were statistically significant patterns, these would not show that faith is unwarranted. To suppose otherwise is to commit one or other (or both) of a pair of errors in reasoning: the genetic and the effective fallacies. The former errs by supposing that because a belief has a cause it cannot also be true; the second by assuming that any claim to truth is undermined by the belief having certain beneficial effects. If asked why I believe that the cube root of 27 is 3 or that the square on the hypotenuse is equal to the sum of the squares on the other two sides, my honest answer is that these are things I was taught. Does the fact that this may be true, or that it might be the case that incidental benefits accrue from such commitments, detract from the justifiability of my beliefs? Clearly not: it is one question why someone believes p, it is another whether p is true or defensible.

I am a professional philosopher who believes in the existence of the God of the Christian creed. My beliefs are the product of a certain upbringing: a devout and charitable mother raised in the warmth of Catholicism; a devoted and serious father raised in the piety of Presbyterianism and subsequently a convert to

Rome; nine years of Jesuit education, followed by twelve years of higher education in art school and university. Is my faith reasonable? Obviously I think it to be so but many, if not most, of my colleagues would deny this. Why is that? Clearly it is not a matter of intelligence. A religious believer is not, as such, any more or any less intellectually competent than an atheist or an agnostic. I suppose I would say that my colleagues have not enjoyed the benefits of membership of a faith community and they would say that I have suffered the indoctrinating effects of one.

Against backgrounds of this and related sorts, is there any way to make progress? What it is reasonable to believe at the most general level is what – all things in one's experience and extended knowledge considered – best makes sense. The older I become, the more I experience, the more I learn, the more I see religion as providing not the content but the context of life. Here is one point at which the secular atheist is at a disadvantage. Those of faith have available to them an account of what things in their particularity and in their generality mean, and they can find both immediate and ultimate point in doing what they can where they can. I am not at all sure that when push comes to shove, the same can be said of the non-believer. So I end where, proverbially, philosophy begins – with the question of the meaning of life, and with the suggestion that only the believer can show that this question is an appropriate one and that it has an answer that being, in the words of the catechism, *to know, to love and to serve God.*

First published entitled "Faith, Reason and Meaning of Life" in *Priests and People*, 12.10, October 1998.

I am not alone
Because from here
may be seen
a splendid garden,
a truly incomparable garden

In this garden
I am an eye
filled with delight;

and the pupil
of this eye
is none other
than my lord

An anonymous inscription in
Ain dar Aisha: a viewing tower
in the Alhambra

Arindam Chakrabarti

THE CLOUD OF PRETENDING

śraddhā mayo'yam puruso, yo yacchraddhah sa eve sah
Bhagavad Gita

... verily, out of your heart you believe in a heart that is
not yours, and you place faith where you do not focus
the glance of either your body or your mind. You discern
your friend's countenance by means of your body ... but
your friend's faith is not appreciated by you, unless there
is in you a reciprocating faith, by which you may believe
what you do not see in him.

St. Augustine, *On Faith in Things Unseen*

Little by little, belief became polluted like air and the
water.

Michel de Certeau, *The Practice of Everyday Life*

The future is an object of wish, will and faith. Faithless wishing
is at best a form of greedy gambling, while faith (that x will
come to pass) without will or endeavor (to bring it about) can be
a lazy pretence of certitude and surrender. The drive of will without
faith leads either to suicidal desperation or to demonic

manipulativeness running amuck with an unyielding illusion of making history. That Truth will triumph and falsehood will lose can never be proved by empirical or logical reasoning. It is an article of faith to be nurtured by the moral ardor of the *heart* (*śraddhām hradayyayā akutyā* – *Rig Veda* X:151-4) and not a piece of CNN news. Yet, without this faith, our collective future is either a set of private fantasies or the dark inevitability of a common doom.

One of the ironies of the present times is that while human beings are obsessed with the future – in their greed for growth, dreams for newer technological wonders, political utopias and fears of global ecological disasters – they also seem to be proudly bereft of faith. As faithless information gatherers, the late twentieth-century educated elite lives under the gloom of futurelessness, of not seeing where one is headed, not knowing what to want next, ready to "wait and see" or, what is equally possible, "wait and not see." The fear of being labelled a "gullible fanatic," a "blind believer," an "irrational zealot" haunts all post-enlightenment human pursuit. Yet the future is not given to observation and experiment. Predictive inferences, like weather reports, give probabilities but for actions to be undertaken unwaveringly, we need more than comparisons of likelihood. We need the leap of faith that what one is striving for will come to pass because it morally *must*. When Arjuna voices the most common human anxiety: "What if, in midway, not having arrived at the goal, torn from both ends, the pursuer of the moral spiritual path of Yoga just perishes like a stray cloud?" (*Bhagavad Gita*, 6:38) Krishna has to restore his faith in no uncertain terms, addressing his friend almost filially, as "my child" (*tāta*): "Partha! Neither here on earth nor hereafter can such a seeker perish. The doer of good, my child, never ends up in a bad way."

Yet not all hearts warm up to such divine assurance. The great book of human life – *Mahabharata* – even after the righteous Yudhisthira has ascended to heaven via a deserved detour through hell, concludes as it were on a note of bitter disappointment with its future unbelieving audience:

Raising my hands, here I cry out and no one listens to me:

From Duty (*dharma*) eventually come both Pleasure (*kama*) and Wealth (*artha*), so why not practice that?

Dharma, of course, does not teach us how to have fun or get rich now or in the future but teaches us how we ought to become worthy of happiness and success. Faith flinches at the sight of unworthy unvirtuous people getting not only richer but sometimes even happier, while the unilateral observer of dharmic duties either waits in line or faces ruin. An enraged Draupadi pours sarcasm on a pacifist pious Son-of-Dharma: "Dharma, I am told, protects all those who observe it, except you whom it does not seem to protect!" So she argues that *now* is not the time to forgive or forbear, it is rather the time to take revenge and wage a war. And the war happens.

Projecting a Draupadi-like image of harrassed Hindutva, the "present" times have been described as the time for a violent reclamation of India's "Vedic" heritage. My conjecture is that such call for action on behalf of a "faith" is actually promoted by a loss of faith in dharma.

Indeed the Mahabharata dictum that Draupadi was sarcastically alluding to, *dharmo rakṣati rakṣitaḥ*, does not mean that dharma can save us only when we protect it from foreign attacks (by burning missionaries or counter-capturing captured places of worship). It means that if we keep morally faithful in our own lives to our own dharmic duties, then Dharma takes care of our own futures. Unfortunately the political fever that ensues from regarding dharma as endangered, needing all the modern aggressive product-promoting marketing techniques to "protect" it from extinction or pollution is, like many forms of aggression, a symptom of insecurity rather than conviction. It leaves little time, patience and contemplative quiet for the actual practice of friendship, compassion and joy, of non-injury, truthfulness, non-theft and control of passions – the real heart of *dharmarakṣa*! As a result, the second part of the *Mahabharata* dictum comes true: *dharma eva hato hanti* (when dharma is violated, it itself becomes a killer).

But there were very good psycho-social reasons for Draupadi's loss of faith and impatience. She could not wait for the indefinite future in which the righteousness of her husbands would bear fruit and the depravity of Duryodhana and his brothers would ripen into their ruin. Krishna saw the truth but, like Tolstoy's God, waited. The dark testing night of exile and humiliation did not seem to be ending. Draupadi wanted to will the future of power and prestige that she wished for, rather than have faith that it will come in the future.

The present, remarked K. C. Bhattacharya, is *known* only as beginning, never as ending. Thus while we are always running into the future as we traverse time at the modest speed of one minute per minute, we never perceive or *know* the future directly. We wait and plan for, worry about, fear, dream, expect, wish, imagine and anticipate the future. We never quite *see* it. If seeing alone is believing for a crass empiricist, then, for such a *carvaka*, there simply is no future to believe in. Yet, right now even the most unthrifty and sceptical hedonistic empiricist in the world is talking about the year 2000 and wondering what it will bring. By the time these words are printed and read, that year would have become the present.

An arbitrary dating system, imposed upon the world by an aggressively other-effacing culture, marks a particular December night in the very near future as the last night of the millennium. The business boom and media hype around this utterly vapid end/ start-of-a-millennium anxiety has now reached almost the level of a worldwide religious frenzy. For some unspelt-out reason, the beginning of the 2000th year of the common era is supposed to be of exceedingly uncommon significance!

The last hundred years have witnessed – along with unthinkable technological advances in making speedy travel, speedy communication across vast distances and speedy massacre of large number of lives possible – a steady *loss of faith* in many spheres of human life and thought. In a recent issue of a popular American Sunday magazine, the last millennium has been termed the Me-millennium. In Indian society this epidemic of egotism has taken the form of a general pessimism about our collective future leading to the shameless mad pursuit of personal financial gain – a sort of ideological switch from Gandhi to Ayn Rand! Though this can be packaged positively as the human being's journey towards greater self-reliance, in the recent past this tendency "no more to depend on any supra-mundane power, no more to rely on Nature's whims but to take personal control of one's own life," has shown its ugly negative face precisely through this loss of faith in the Other: the divine Other, the species other, the cultural other, and indeed even the individual other. This faithless hubris often expresses itself in slogans like "I have confidence in ME!"

Simple faith in God had started to go out of fashion already by the end of the last century. Awe at the deeds of Rama, Krishna or Durga is now being replaced by awe about imaginary aliens and Star-trek characters. Faith in the unquestionable superiority of ethical over egotistic living has also withered away. Finally, faith in the possibility of a peaceful co-flourishing of the plurality of traditions and religions within a single civil society seems to be waning as well. From the Vedic announcement, "One is the Real, but the learned describe It in many different ways," through the Jaina philosophy of Alternative True Views, this faith in plurality without rivalry of faiths seems to have survived in India, until the partition, and its aftermath of riots and rapes, mocked and mauled Gandhi's chant "*Ishwara Allah tera nam.*" This last decline of hope has now marked religious faith itself as a destructive rather than constructive force, because blind faith, apparently, has too often led to mass conversion, genocide, communal revenge-spirals and the politics of hate.

In this short paper I cannot address the hard and complex issue of choice of faith from among those various faiths that a multicultural society seems to open up for us and our choice-loving children. I am not even sure that faith can be chosen. I am only concerned with the need to have *faith in general in one's own tradition's ethical ideals* and the necessity of having a hopeful heart inspite of an unbelieving brain. I do want to make three points about conflict of faiths and its alleged potential for violence.

(a) It is not faith but lack of faith which usually turns a community violent. If Hindus really believed that Rama or Shiva is omnipotent and omnipresent then they would not have taken up arms or the microphones to protect Rama or *mimic* past usurpers of Hindu sacred spaces in trying to rehabilitate Rama.

Swami Vivekananda was told something to this effect by the divine Mother when he thought to himself, amidst the ruins of Khir Bhavani temple in Kashmir, that had he been alive at the time he would have protected the original temple from Muslim invaders.

(b) Faith in practice, at least of the kind that is more festive, more inclusive and which celebrates diversity, has been a source of tolerance and syncretism rather than separatism. Devout Muslims have sung *"Hari Om tat Sat"* or *"Vande nanda kumaram"* while Hindus have worshipped in dargahs of great Pirs. Analysing the potentials of popular faith as a means of preserving a rooted religious but non-sectarian public culture, Rustom Bharucha ends his searching critique of modern Indian secularism (*The Question of Faith*, Orient Longman, 1993) with these remarks: "Secularists have a lot to learn from the idioms of tolerance embedded in every religious faith. As Ashish Nandy rightly points out, one can only hope that the state-systems in South Asia may learn something about religious tolerance from everyday Hinduism, Islam, Buddhism and Sikhism." It is only state-making ambitions using Hinduism and Islam that generate hatred. True, there are elements, like the pollution taboos about food in Hinduism and the anti-idolatry animus in Christianity and Islam, that create tensions between communities. But there has also been room for poets like Kazi Nazrul Islam who are proud to be Muslim devotees of Mother Kali or social reformers like Brahmabandhav Upadhyaya who roam around in ochre robe as Catholic Vedantin which proves that the actual practice of these faiths leaves enough room for wonderfully shaded areas in their borders.

(c) It is not just politicization of religions that makes faith wear a mask of hate. Intellectual and rational reflection on religious experience which gives rize to theologies also imposes its rigidly drawn doctrinal boundaries upon faith. Now in every other sphere of social action and policy, the dialogical tools of determination, debate and argumentation are excellent for an open society. But spiritual or mystical experiences are better communicated through poetry, music and direct human interaction rather than through philosophical systematizations. Thus while Ramakrishna and Keshab Chandra Sen would sing and meditate together, the Hindu and

Brahmo pandits may have been fighting about the permissibility of worshipping Gods in idols.

The philosophical attempts at finding out the universal spiritual core of conflicting creeds are usually looked upon with great suspicion by theologians and philosophers of every creed. A recent Sanskrit monograph by Professor Govind Chandra Pande called *Ekam Sad Viprā Bahudhā Vadanti* is an astute and responsible defence of direct spiritual experience as the shared epistemology of all the world's great religions. This tiny but intricately argued book shows how a basically unificatory non-dualistic religious experience gets interpreted into incompatible ontologies and religious dogmas at different historical junctures due to different social and environmental conditions. Thus, once again, an age old Advaitic stance expresses itself in Pande's categorization of the core experience! Pande's book, one may say, is meant for intellectuals. But one has seen less dispute between Buddhist, Sikh, Hindu and Sufi saints than one has seen between Buddhist, Hindu, Muslim and Christian theologians and philosophers.

This last point should not mislead us into a general denunciation of rational philosophical discourse and a promotion only of hymn-chanting and mass meditation-camps (although I do think *kirtans* and devotional music have had, and will always have, a major role to play in bringing out the integrative rather than divisive side of faiths). Indian religions have had the richest traditions of uncensored philosophical debate which have kept even the common public always aware of the falsifiability of religious *theories*. Even the Rig Veda celebrates the spirit of questioning and debate. A healthy dose of scepticism keeps the sage Dirghatamas ready for the spiritual awakening after that dark night of unknowing that his name suggests. Such a doubting, debating, honest inquiry is quite compatible with the simple moral faith which keeps us hoping: "there must be an answer!" The not-knowing goes on in the intellect while the assurance that one shall know one day possesses the heart.

The Sanskrit word for faith, *Śraddhā*, is etymologically connected with the English word "cardiac": *śrat* means the heart. In faith the heart finds its resting place. A mere intellectual heartless existence is bound to be wedded to scepticism. Russell was haunted by such pure intellectualism and its attendant faithlessness all his life until, as he claimed, he found solace in a loving heart.

Humans cannot live by scepticism and relativism alone. "This human person is made of faith, you are what you have faith in" says the first epigraph I have lifted from the *Bhagavad Gita*. Faith is particularly crucial as an epistemic constituent of that attitude towards the future which we call "lovingly looking forward to without rational or empirical ground of expectation." St. Augustine gives two excellent arguments for the indispensability of faith in this sense. First, without such reasonless faith human relations would break down. Children would not recognize or depend upon parents because there is no evidence for most of us that these are our parents, and no guarantee that they will take care of us. Friends without *faith* would not trust each other because friendship can only be felt by faith.

Second, the search for a knowledgeable teacher (since I find myself in a state of ignorance) requires that we trust someone unknowingly, on pain of a vicious circle of needing to know what this teacher knows, etc. "For how will we fools be able to find a wise man? ... the fool does not know wisdom and, not knowing it, cannot recognize it elsewhere ... For this immense difficulty in our search for religion, then only God can supply the remedy. And unless we believe (without knowing with reason) that he exists and assists human souls we ought not even look for the true religion itself" (St. Augustine, *Advantage of believing* 13, 28).

Such a paradox did not threaten young Nachiketa (whose name meant, with humility, "one who does not know") when faith possessed him, *śraddhā āviveśa* (*Katha Upanishad* 12). Death, of whom he asked "Is there life after death or not, since some say there is and some say there is not?" tried his best to dodge the question. But Nachiketa, although he had an existential doubt about the nature of the soul, had unflinching faith that Death knows the answer to his question and that he will not go back without that answer.

But how did Nachiketa gain such faith? Well, he detected bad faith in his father Vājaśravas. Vājaśravas was pompously performing an all-giving sacrifice. But he was not actually giving all he had. He was giving out old cows which could no longer breed or give milk or even chew grass anymore. Nachiketa sensed that his father was religious but faithless. Had he really been giving away all he had, he should have given away his son, myself, one of his most precious possessions. So with simple faith he asked his father "To whom are you giving me?" When the father felt pestered by the son's persistent query he yelled at him "I give you to Death." So, to Death he went.

The syndrome which now plagues us, as it afflicts Indian society, now facing technological globalization and already wallowing in economic liberalization, is not lack of religious zeal. Temples inside and outside India are thriving, garish religious television programmes are endlessly popular, gurus and priests carry cell-phones, ashrams have web-pages, and to crown it all, successful politics is, more than ever before, unabashedly religious. Yet somewhere there is a deep dearth of faith in all such religious regeneration.

It has been upon this phenomenon of faithless religiosity that I mainly wished to dwell. I think the proudly Hindu part of Indian society is suffering from what I would like to call the Vājaśravas Syndrome. We deliver speeches and give our Sunday mornings to TV-watching and donate our NRI excess income to charities in the cause of Hindu revival, but we keep our children in English medium schools for education and thereafter Americanized IIT education, eventually to be packed off to the States. Very soon our frankly un-understanding children will detect this lack of faith in us. Let us hope that the real faith possesses their pure hearts too, as it did Nachiketa's.

We are afraid that our egotistically defined religious culture would meet its death if we did not rally for it and only pretended to perform many sacrifices! Let us hope our future Nachiketas will not be afraid and insecure like us and would actually want to meet with death and get whatever boons they want, without being waylaid by the lure of the "good life" defined by whatever terms prevailing of consumer marketing.

Donald Eichert

Diminishing Spirit

With every passing year it becomes harder to believe. It strains credulity, for instance, that once, while public awareness was focussed elsewhere – on the Independence struggle, the expulsion of the British and the ensuing failed experiment for an egalitarian society – even while all that was playing itself out, India's spiritual life was unusually rich and colorful. Great figures, attained men and women all, strode the land. Those who were known, like Ramana Maharshi, like Shirdi Sai Baba, left the scene half a century and more ago. One doesn't even hear about the others: Sri Yashoda Mai, Brahmagya Mai, Harihar Baba, Somwari Baba ... right down to Nisargadutta Maharaj and Sri Madhava Ashish (the English *sadhu* who left us just two years ago).

These men and women flowered in India, led lives that should rightly be the stuff of legend, interacted with high-profile figures in significant encounters that would bemuse the biographer. Who remembers them now? The sad truth is, the middle class of today doesn't want to hear about our saints. And if they do stumble on some anecdote they can make nothing of it in the current context.

It was no pack of lies concocted by eccentric travel-writers that earned India a reputation for spirituality. For over three millennia men and women reached attainment here, founded occult schools and recorded their insights in what has come down to us as scripture. This tradition survived invasion, spoliation, colonization and evangelism. (At the World Islamic Conference in London, 1980, there was screened a documentary called *The Inner Life* wherein it was remarked, in the voice-over, that it was in India that Muslim mysticism found an ambience congenial to its expression.) The question that confronts us is: Will the tradition survive the onslaught of television and Western-style consumerism?

People concerned about the decline in the ethos draw comfort from the popularity of the televised *Mahabharata*. Good, so far as it goes. But many a viewer leads a double life, his psyche compartmentalized according to the context of the moment. It's a common enough human failing to sport different masks, reflecting different integrations, according to social demands: worldly, westernized, efficient in the office; pliable, obsequious with elders; alternately gruff and cuddly *en père de famille*; camel-faced at funerals and on religious, corporate and family occasions. It's hard to be one person, and just where the spiritual component can be expected to find a face in this flux takes some figuring.

An outsider could be forgiven for concluding that spirituality is no more representative of modern India than Khajuraho – less, indeed! While from year to year religious festivals are progressively reduced to social statements, the middle class, particularly English-speaking, alienated and ambitious, digresses into whatever passes for "high life" at their income level. In this article I shall bring speculative psychology to bear on the question: How did the Indian upwardly mobile professional ("yuppie") get this way?

But first, a glance at the broader picture, at the 800 million Indians who don't exist for us. Village India is changing but the chasm that has opened up between its lifestyle and that of the well-off urbanite is seismic in scale. Up to Independence there was nothing like it: the contact had remained. However autocratic, the princely ruler and the *zamindaar* lived symbiotically close to the villager. The city-dweller would drag his cot out on the roof to wait out the June nights, the *gowala* milked his cow under the *bahu's* eye. (Doubtless this goes on yet in some small towns.) *Sadhus* begged door to door and some of them were *sadhaks*. The ochre robe was much more than a disguise.

Like this, the educated elite stayed in touch with the realities of rural India, leaving the door open for wonderful improbabilities. For example, an ailing Swami Vivekananda, offered hospitality in a Ghazipur home, performed *kanya puja* to Monica, his host's daughter, who later became Sri Yashoda Mai. Such anecdotes will shortly die out along with the generation that still harbors them.

Down the centuries it was benighted village India that produced *mahatmas*, the living correlative of the perennial wisdom that spawned Brahminism, Buddhism, Jainism and Sikhism, fostered Sufism and nurtured great religious music and the most profoundly-conceived sculpture in the world. Before we turn the page on that great heritage we should ask ourselves what we stand to gain by way of compensation.

The late Piloo Mody judged India "a nation 75 per cent illiterate, and the balance uneducated." Without checking the percentage, without defining "educated," we can perhaps agree that India now boasts an educated class that is much more than just literate. Is that just where the tectonic plate slid under? Our question is: What happened to the psyche of the educated Indian? Let us approach the question obliquely, believing that novel angles will yield unsuspected insights.

Asked his reaction to a Sviatoslav Richter piano recital, Canadian pianist Glenn Gould replied: "Quite the best piano-playing I have ever heard." It was no commendation, because "piano-playing" was Gould's term for showmanship at the expense of music making. A pianist who salvaged Bach from decades of sentiment, Gould recorded the *Goldberg Variations* not once but twice, because, he said, his first rendition in the 1950s was marred by "a lot of piano-playing." His perception that many concert artistes were more concerned with acting out a romantic role than serving the composer, represented what might be called a paradigm shift.

As soon as one saw what Gould was getting at when he condemned "piano-playing," one began to apply a similar analysis to writing, to painting and the cinema. With the proliferation of the media, more and more normally artistic activity was submitted to formula treatment. The dominance of cinema and television led writers to think in visual terms. As serious a writer as Solzhenitsyn could interlard a novel – *August 1914* – with explicit film script, like the scene of the windmill burning. Less conscientious novelists wrote "the book of the film" they envisaged cashing in on. How else explain the epic treatment accorded to the truck driver in *The Horse Whisperer?*

All this "piano-playing," if I may extrapolate Gould's term, brings to mind the slogan of his fellow-countryman, Marshall MacLuhan. "The medium is the message" supplied at once the maxim for the current art scene and a diagnosis of its bankruptcy. If the medium becomes the message the resulting construct is culturally empty. It is the packaging without the product, which comes frighteningly close to a description of the supermarket. What's inside the wrapping is your old toothpaste, of course, though it will be conceded that much of the contents of the packets barely answer the description printed thereon.

It's not all that odd that the world of music should provide a word for this bamboozlement of the consumer. Music has long been an occasion for *tamasha*, with the soloist as hero and the music as a kind of backdrop. What else is the cadenza in the typical concerto, where the soloist shows off his skills at the expense of the aesthetics?

This is what is called role identification. Consider any yuppie on his first day in a new job. To please his boss he bends his efforts to identify with his new role. This applies pretty well across the white-collar class. It applies heroically to the armed forces, else how do you persuade a young man to walk into machine-gun fire? It applies to a wide range of humble earners, from *paanwalas* to restaurant bouncers. There are a few noble professions where role identification, if not altogether absent, is evidently eclipsed by the importance of the work in hand and the necessity of exercising real skill: surgery, bus-driving spring to mind. Against this, a vast number of earners in our transitional society are acting out a sort of dream: I am a reporter, I am an actor, I am a car salesman. In Bombay there is a population of "wannabe" stars out of all proportion to the possible work.

The obvious motivation for making like an actress or like a policeman is to earn money. But it doesn't explain the identification, it doesn't get inside the subject's consciousness. What goes on inside when the new CEO of such and such a firm assumes the mantle? There seems to be some kind of reflexive awareness. Wow, I'm the boss/have my own command/dance Giselle tonight/walked across Antarctica. When, in Britain's darkest hour, Churchill became prime minister he ended a momentous day filled with satisfaction, confident he could discharge his new role adequately. Among other preparations to that end, we learn, he rehearsed his historic speeches in front of a mirror.

A reflective but weak-minded person, genuinely moved by, say, a religious performance, can fall prey to the thought: "I'm very moved!" The tragedy of someone thinking "I'm moved!" is that it kills the feelings, replacing them with self-congratulation. Instead of being carried on a wave of feeling, spontaneous before great art, great nature and certain human interactions, the subject derives satisfaction from monitoring his own mechanisms.

The incidence of the kind of psychic tendencies we have been discussing is all the greater in our media-crazed culture. Genuine emotion gives way to showing off. Acting, of all the performing arts, is the stuff of idolatry. "Look ... tears in's eyes," but as Hamlet, tormented by his inability to feel strongly enough for decisive action, reflects: "What's Hecuba to him, and he to Hecuba?"

We are told that tragedy "purges the soul by pity and terror," and there are two opinions whether that kind of purgation is a good thing. Socrates didn't think so. It is interesting that the Greek tragedians wore masks, as if to depersonalize the emotion. The author of the *Natyashastra* knew that *abhinaya* could not only express emotion, but awaken it in the performer. The side-to-side movements of the neck and eyes could actually arouse feelings of devotion to the deity the *devadasi* honored in the temple images. This may be regarded as the opposite end of the spectrum to what Gould called "piano-playing." The *devadasi*, using tried techniques, arouses genuine emotion; the "piano-player," in Gould's pejorative sense, uses tried techniques to attract the audience's admiration to himself. In the process, emotion goes out of the window.

I have floated the idea that the causation underlying the "piano-playing" in different walks of life has to do with role identification. In the performing arts this means playing to the gallery. In the workplace it means self-consciously adopting the paraphernalia of the trade, the patter, the tone of voice, etc. For many younger people it means playing to an audience of parents or imagined elders – a sort of Walter Mitty posturing. There are those for whom the interaction with an audience is so obsessive that the subject can't *not* act. The compulsion to milk an imaginary subject's experience for a feeling we have lost the power to tap directly is said to yield vicarious emotion. In the absence of theatrical conventions such second-hand emotion is seen for the absurdity it is.

I now propose to deploy a terminology that I believe helps one to understand these convolutions of the psyche: Gurdjieff's doctrine of the three "brains" or "centers." Those familiar with the Gurdjieff movement will recall that he referred to Man as "three-brained" or "three-centered." These three brains or centers corresponded to thinking, feeling and moving or physical activity, respectively. One of Gurdjieff's contributions to the understanding of the psyche was the insight that much psychic illness reflects what he called "the wrong work of the centers," meaning that, due to one cause or another, one center habitually performs the functions properly performed by another center. According to this way of looking at the problem, much of the emotional dysfunction in our lives is the result of "feeling with the thinking center" and "thinking with the feeling center." For example, one who is distracted by the thought "I'm very moved" tends to sacrifice emotion at the altar of an intellectual self-appraisal. The thinking center trespasses. Again, one who lets the feeling center interfere with the moving center while driving a car is a dangerous driver while the state lasts. And we are all familiar with the destructive effects of letting feelings dictate our decisions that properly are the domain of the intellect or commonsense.

Since it was proposed in Gurdjieff's Moscow lectures in 1913, this conceptualization has proved extraordinarily fruitful in the diagnosis of psychic dysfunction. Let us apply it to "piano-playing." Making music is an activity that enlists more than one "center": the moving center plays (or sings) the actual notes; the thinking center lends form to the music; and (if there is some degree of mastery) the feeling center communicates emotive content by the expression of aesthetic values. What happens in "piano-playing" in Gould's sense is that the thinking center goes off on a side-trip. While keeping the show on the road, pausing at the right places, regulating the dynamics, the intellect allows itself to be distracted by the idea "I am playing the piano." This inevitably affects the performance by interfering with the moving center's work and distorting the emotive message of the music. If this attitude becomes habitual, the performer's style is corrupted by it. A pianist becomes notorious for his body language, the dramatic lifting of the hands unnecessarily high above the keyboard (interference of the thinking center with the moving center). Sentimentality infects and cheapens the aesthetic content, so that the player earns a reputation for schmalz.

Mindless action knows no cultural barrier: it's easy to recognize. Mechanicality in the performing arts isn't of course strictly mindless: by the three-center model it would describe activity entirely governed by the moving center, whereas good music-making, I suggest, requires the participation of all three "brains." I gave up attending Hindustani music sessions quarter of a century ago because in a dozen concerts there would scarcely be one "high." That was a subjective reaction. But in the interval at a Bismillah Khan recital I told one critic: "The first sentence of your review can read: 'Bismillah Khan played in his sleep!'" "Now you are beginning to understand our music," he said. As to Carnatic music, much of it prompts the archetypally South Indian question What is there? Hearing Mahalingam's flute for the first time, the young Amjad Ali Khan commented: *Yeh aatman ki baat hai.* (It is to do with the atman.) I have heard M. D. Ramanathan, I have watched Balasaraswati and heard her sing, movingly. So I know there can be something "there." My question is: How often? When do the thinking and feeling centers come to the aid of the moving center in the *raagam, tanam* and *pallavi?*

I have been using music as a metaphor for the still, sad music of humanity. Now I want to apply the concept of the three "brains" or "centers" to the life around us, specifically to the lifestyle of the educated middle class. For starters, I invoke another useful Gurdjieff idea, which can be summed up thus: Whenever one culture imitates another it adopts the worst features of that other culture, to the neglect of the good ones. The obvious reaction is that this is an exaggeration. India surely didn't imitate only the worst features of the West. That's the good news.

The bad news is that this nation took on a lot of stuff uncritically. Worse, when they import a concept, Indians have a flair for missing the point, for getting the appearance right at the expense of the function or essence. The beer is full of glycerine, except on the west coast the bread's like biting into a face towel. Everything is for looks. Apples are supposed to be red, aren't they? So India gets stuck with the so-called Delicious, which makes like cottonwool after two days. (A good russet apple stays three months.) One could extend the list indefinitely: garish furniture, the vulgar celebration of imported holidays in hotels and restaurants, the craze for imported electronics, the obsession with "green cards," never mind the years of homesickness and alienation. Presiding over all this is the uncritically accepted idea that foreign is better.

But all this is small potatoes compared with the inroads on the life of the mind. India didn't exactly import them, the nation had thrust upon it the missionary schools which, besides providing a good education, mostly English-medium, colored the whole contemporary ethos. "We're missionaries," the chemistry master at one of the big Nainital schools told me, apparently in reaction to my un-Christian aura. The fact is, for generations the missionary schools have turned out English-speaking citizens who, although unconverted to the Christian rite, have at the thinking level lost their family religion, at least if it happened to be Hindu. Such generalizations suffer from the weakness of all casual empiricism. But having known a hundred or so products of the missionary schools, I venture to share the impression that in their public integration the missionary school alumni are metaphysical materialists: they think that ultimate reality is matter. If I were John Maynard Keynes I would probably set up an equation: *mythology + mythology = materialism.*

That is, if you superimpose the western Christian mythology on Hindu mythology they cancel one another out. And because the common man's metaphysical beliefs, if any, rest on a foundation of mythology, if the foundation is destroyed, or neutralized, the superstructure disappears, or sinks into the subconscious. In the absence of a belief in the Divine you get, if not atheism, an unquestioned acceptance of sensory experience as the touchstone of reality, which outside the philosophy departments, implies materialism.

That this naive materialism is the working philosophy of the urban anglophone Indian is borne out by most aspects of his current lifestyle, whether at work or at leisure. It finds explicit confirmation in the media. Under the impulse of Gresham's Law, that bad currency drives out good, the bright boys and girls who key in our newspapers and saturate our television screens inexorably, day by day, mire our culture ever deeper.

It may be said, by the way, that the "materialism" of Indians is what is most noticed by those foreigners who have not been grabbed by the talk of "spirituality": the dowry murders, the oriental splendor (read vulgarity) of weddings, the dishonest traders, all presided over by the bureaucrat with palm outstretched. I shall only say that this kind of materialism is not the metaphysical kind. Spiritual beliefs are quite compatible, alas, with crass display of wealth, and the unscrupulous quest of it, in the sense that the two states of mind coexist in the same body. It takes a pretty high level of integration for one's spiritual beliefs to find expression in an austere lifestyle.

The unconscious conspiracy to bury India's spiritual heritage which the lifestyle of the English-speaking Indian corroborates, owes much to satellite TV, something to the penetration of the multinationals and much, no doubt, to the rebellion of the younger generation against the family traditions. But the ground had been prepared for this degeneration by the output of mostly bright anglophone young Indians whose religious and cultural roots were axed in the missionary schools. It is not a question of articulating atheism: it is a question of thinking like a westerner. The typical westerner – one might say the typical late twentieth century man or woman – believes in nothing that's not written about in Western newspapers. That covers a lot of ground, admittedly, including topics like the possibility of life in other solar systems, with the overtone of mystery, as in *Star Trek*. But what is the integration that supports these beliefs? If pressed to state his ultimate beliefs, the westerner will come out with some formula that reduces to materialism (metaphysical variety). Pressed further he will often make a wistful reference to half-forgotten possibilities – "a sense of something far more deeply interfused" – but that is not a belief, that is the depth of the psyche protesting the ideological burden of materialism.

What concerns us is that, almost imperceptibly, this response has become the public posture of the urban educated Indian. It is mirrored in the media. Faced with reference to anything remotely supernatural, current newsroom conventions, dutifully imbibed from the West, dictate that the matter be treated condescendingly, with a nod and a wink, as it were. Thus one newspaper runs a series about encounters with ghosts, but the tone is nostalgic: "this is what it could have been like" or "remember when ghosts were common currency?"

This in a country where the ordinary man worships ghosts! This is how far the missionary schools have carried the day. From believing in ghosts – which, however humble a community, *exist* – the urban educated Indian, in his workplace integration, believes in nothing. This is the land of village Hinduism, which is more like Japanese Shinto than Hindu nationalists would like to admit. The *devta*, like the Shinto medium, periodically becomes possessed by a departed soul that draws power from the offerings of devotees who worship at the local shrine. If there is a *devta* to mediate, the devotees get verbal answers to their questions. If not, they may get help in other ways. The power of these stranded "deities" in rural India every now and then makes headlines. Since the practice of importuning them has colored history for 3,000 years from Delphi to Hokkaido it is not something one need brush under the carpet.

To be "with it" was it altogether necessary to junk all this venerable lore? Ghost talk isn't spirituality, of course; it's spiritism. It is not virtuous, being propelled by selfishness. Still, there is a tenuous connection with religion for, as a great man said, if there are ghosts, God is a possibility. That is, there exists consciousness without a physical support: then metaphysical materialism is wrong.

The missionary schools wanted to replace the edifice itself, not just the basement. They wanted to replace the Hindu pantheon with their own Trinity, and the result, I have suggested, was a turn-off vis-a-vis religion in all recensions. For unformed minds that had not been awed by the Trimurti at Elephanta or a thousand other temples that evoke the Eternal, the result of substituting one mythology for another was not to unleash an internal conflict so much as to overload the system. As to the majestic higher reaches of Indian thought, boys and girls wouldn't have been touched by the *Upanishads*, Shankaracharya and the heritage of yogis' teachings. So that, at the thinking level, India was left a legacy of unreflecting scepticism.

But this airy structure was reared in defiance of family values, comprising *ishta, gotra*, caste, *biraadari, tirths*, saints' days and the national epics. The lessons instilled by the grandfather-grandson *parampara*, the tales from the *Ramayana* learnt at grandpa's knee, would have left an impression well-nigh indelible. Add to this the domestic calendar: thread ceremonies, *pujas*, weddings, women's fast days and the religious festivals with the excitement of Diwali, the burning of Ravana, the color-throwing at Holi. All this would have conditioned the child irreversibly, unless some quirk of his nature induced one of those revulsions that tend to punctuate one's adolescence. So that when the child was plunged into the milieu of a residential missionary school, from the evangelist's point of view the damage had already been done: the child was beyond saving.

What the missionaries did manage to do was engineer a kind of split. School and university over, the intellect hived off to do its own thing in the psychedelic ambience of liberalized urban

India, where, in the more hyped-up professions, you could buy a new car with two months' salary. The emotions underpinning this joyride meanwhile stayed at home. Far from having the best of both worlds, the Indian yuppie has neither, because he's not all there himself. This mildly schizoid predicament perhaps accounts for the manic air of much that goes on in the megalopolises: the hysterical advertising, the obsession with boutiques and models – *models*! – the expensive restaurants serving imitation food.

Part of the benefit of the thinking and feeling centers functioning together is that they, as it were, monitor each other. There is a mutual curbing of excess: emotionalism and intellectualism – both pejorative terms, incidentally. But if the adman leaves his feelings at home, just what has he got to work with in his fantasy world? His English-medium schooling and his moving center. If the moving center intrudes on the creative process in the absence of the normative impact of feeling you get some pretty hairy products. It takes the thinking and the feeling centers working in concert to recognize unconscious projections and assess their relevance to the task in hand. In the absence of such checks and balances what you get overall is mechanicality.

In terms of working integration the typical Westerner is better equipped than the Indian yuppie. "He has got his act together." He is a professed materialist whose simplistic world-picture ought to forestall internal conflicts. His idea of reality is based on an impenetrable misunderstanding of contemporary science. But such emotion as he has at his disposal is often hijacked by neurosis, manifesting in sentimentality, infantile religiosity, road rage, maudlin jingoism, etc. In this brittle psychic environment the Westerner's unreasoning materialism tends to be corroded by millennarian fantasies and a sneaking taste for the occult. To surf the Western media is to be confronted with the mores of Gibbon's *Decline and Fall of the Roman Empire*. And that classic, mind you, is the (no doubt unacknowledged) model for much of what goes on in the name of being "with it."

In this article I have suggested some perspectives on the religious disaffection of the urban Indian and proposed an aetiology. Any reader who doesn't acknowledge the problem – the degeneration of the culture among the educated urban elite – will, of course, have found the procedure pointless. As to the diagnosis, I have brought to bear some categories unknown to orthodoxy: the classification of thinking, feeling and moving as distinct functions of the psycho-physical organism. But there is no orthodoxy in psychology. Meanwhile Gurdjieff's analysis offers an insight into the mechanicality that afflicts Indian life as we enter the new millenium.

Alok Pandey

To a Greater Dawn

Human life is a journey. But it is a journey in a very special sense. We move as if on an uncharted ocean, without map or even compass to steer by. It does not follow the logical course we would like it to take. We want one thing but another happens, we aim for one result but another is given to us. Unforeseen happenings make a mockery of our efforts while phantoms of the past drag us into the backwaters. The present slips away. The gift of daybreak soon pales into the shadows of night. Sometimes we land on rich ports, sometimes in lonely and hostile lands and sometimes our fragile ship simply dashes against the rocks and sinks. We neither know where our journey began nor where we are going, not even why or how we boarded the ship to sail Time's sea.

A candle flare of light trembles before the storm, surrounded by the immense darkness of not knowing. This is our own ordinary, customary view of life. And the Persian poet expressed this hollow sense of meaninglessness:

> Ah make the most of what we yet may spend
> Until we too into the dust descend.

> Dust unto dust and under dust to lie
> Sans song, sans singer, sans wine, sans end.

However, this common view is not the only view, for there are a few who have gazed far out to the distant horizons. Wordsworth in one of his sublime moments declared

> Our birth is but a sleep and forgetting
> The soul that rises with us, our life's star
> That had elsewhere its setting and cometh from afar
> Not in entire forgetfulness, and not in utter nakedness
> But trailing clouds of glory do we come
> From God, who is our home....

A few eagle-winged spirits have climbed high beyond the mist to the golden orb of the sun. A few have dared to question the darkness of ignorance and plunged deep into the springs of life to seek the light.

Thus, we find, we have a double view of life, or a double life-track, so to say, of which the outer seems to course from the dark womb of birth to the dark jaws of death, all the while groping for survival. Running parallel to this and supporting it, albeit secretly, is another track, aspiring from light to greater light, from dawn to greater dawn, with death, darkness, suffering or pain as interregnum and phase. It is an instinct which risks all, dares the impossible and attains it. To hold these two lines together and to bridge the gap there is the mixed tissue of our human mind and its psychology. It is a middle region, full of our hopes and fears, vain successes and glorious failures, the transient sap of pleasure and pain. It is a fragile bridge thrown across the two parallel heights. And human life can well be described as a journey that tries to cross this bridge, unceasingly.

Life, in the total sense, is an effort to bridge the gap between what we are and what we aspire to be, between our limited present actuality and our latent potentiality. All life, in fact, is an effort of nature to manifest and realize with increasing fullness that which is latent in it. The caterpillar holds in its cocoon the magnificent butterfly, the bud conceals the rose, a tiny seed the oak. So it is with the human race. The imperfect animal start of the human race holds within itself the possible birth of great and luminous gods. Our limitations contain the transcendence that has yet to awake. Our finite smallness is only a self-limitation of the infinite, and death a passage to timelessness. That is why, whatever be our present state, there is something in us that never tires of aspiring. Sri Aurobindo affirms this aspiration thus:

> The earliest preoccupation of man in his awakened thoughts and, as it seems, his inevitable and ultimate preoccupation — for it survives the longest periods of scepticism and returns after every banishment — is also the highest which his thought can envisage. It manifests itself in the divination of godhead, the impulse towards perfection, the search after pure Truth and unmixed Bliss, the sense of a secret immortality.
>
> *The Life Divine*

It is here then, that the root of life's malady lies, the dissonance between what we are and what we aspire to be. Where shall we escape from this discontent? What governance, what ideology, what system of law and social administration can help us to outgrow our inner limitation? Material science can conquer outer space, but what will help us conquer our inner spaces? We can modify behavior with drugs and lull ourselves into self-oblivion. But what will make us realize our own intimations of the luminous wisdom, truth and love? Law and polity can create a mechanical order but cannot deliver the key to harmonize conflicts. Reason, ethics, codes and creeds may give a workable social life but will not help us towards an understanding of our oneness with all existence.

This is not to say that science, ethics, law, polity, philosophy and religion have no place. Every human effort directed sincerely towards perfecting life has its rightful place in the march of time. However, it would be an error to suppose that the human race can solve the problem of its existence through outer means alone. Sri Aurobindo again points to this in *The Life Divine*:

> A perfected human world cannot be created by men or

composed of men who are themselves imperfect. Even if all our actions are scrupulously regulated by education or law or social or political machinery, what will be achieved is a regulated pattern of minds, a fabricated pattern of lives, a cultivated pattern of conduct; but a conformity of this kind cannot change, cannot re-create the man within, it cannot carve or cut out a perfect soul or a perfect thinking man or a perfect or growing living being. One can indeed help the being to grow ... but the growth must still come from within it, determining from there what shall be made of these influences and forces, and not from outside. This is the first truth that our creative zeal and aspiration have to learn, otherwise all our human endeavor is foredoomed to turn in a futile circle and can end only in a success that is a specious failure.

The psychology of yesterday laid a great stress on survival, but adjustment or adaptation is not the whole sense of life. If that were so, life would have stopped with the perfectly adaptable protozoa and failed to climb beyond the plant or spread its wings in the sky. The psychology of today still labors under the shadow of the past and its heavy leaning on the material basis of all phenomena. But signs are already appearing of what may come tomorrow: the emerging interest in the discipline of yoga, the growing interest in the science of consciousness, the search for alternate paradigms, even a return to a more holistic approach. The psychology of the future will surely see a breakthrough in the limits of our perception and understanding, of thought, feeling and action. However clumsy and hesitating our human start, the infant strivings of the soul in us must mature into a being luminous and beautiful.

It is in this secret growth that the significance of every crisis lies. The key for future psychology is not survival alone but evolution. And the key to this evolution does not lie in manipulating our outer environment with gadgets and machinery but in shedding our inner walls. Each human crisis becomes therefore a pointer towards some yet unconquered limitation in us. Thus seen, we begin to grow into another way of living. Instead of breaking down under the burden of life and its countless challenges, we strive to conquer it. Instead of stunning our sense of pain with sleeping pills we confront the suffering with a wide vision. The anomalies of life cannot be mastered by the divided and dividing ego in us but only by the all harmonizing faculty of the soul.

It is here that spiritual life steps in to bridge the hiatus between our outer, limited and narrow existence and a wider vaster, truer living. True spiritual life begins when this unconscious quest of life towards the goal of its own fulfillment becomes conscious. This awareness of our seeking and inadequate finding no doubt brings suffering and pain but taken rightly it also opens the door of a greater possibility. This possibility is the ascent of life out of our blind animal urges through the ignorant human beings that we are, towards the divine, towards which we climb.

This conscious and deliberately willed evolution towards our own higher actualization is what is meant by spirituality. Such a spiritual life is not contradicted by life but is rather co-terminus with it, nay, its very fulfillment. For it is in the secret sanctuary of our being and in the silence of the spirit, within and above, that we find the key to our seeking. Here is the peace that surpasses all understanding, the delight ever in possession of itself. To know and live in it and by it is the whole essence and meaning of spiritual life, and the goal and purpose of life itself. As Sri Aurobindo observes:

> In the right view, both of life and of yoga, all life is either consciously or subconsciously a yoga. For we mean by this term a methodized effort towards self-perfection by the expression of the potentialities latent in the being and a union of the human existence we see partially expressed in man and in the cosmos. But all life, when we look behind its appearances, is a vast yoga of nature attempting to realize her perfection in an ever increasing expression of her potentialities and to unite herself with her own divine reality.
>
> *The Synthesis of Yoga*

Of course, the spiritual life being spoken of here has nothing to do with the world-shunning ascetic who, often seized by an impulse of personal salvation, exiles himself into another brighter world. Nor has it anything to do with that which regards life upon earth as a dream of vanity and an illusion. Neither is the term adequate if we mean to understand by it a credal religious dogma, a blind ritualistic adherence or exalted emotional and pietistic fervor or even a rational ethic with a touch of humanitarianism and philanthropy. Spiritual life has its own means and methods of knowing, understanding, sensing, living, and yes, of acting upon and experiencing the world. It can use the mind, but is not limited by it.

> A spiritual idea is a power, but only when it is both inwardly and outwardly creative.... Undoubtedly, spiritual truth exists eternally beyond, independent of us in the heavens of the Spirit; but it is of no avail for humanity here; it does not become truth of earth, truth of life, until it is lived. The divine perfection is always there above us; but for man to become divine and lead outwardly the divine life is what is meant by spirituality; all lesser meanings given to the word are inadequate fumblings or impostures.
>
> Sri Aurobindo, *The Human Cycle*

To live in the spirit then, is the culmination offered to us, the resolution to the enigma and paradox of life, towards which humanity has toiled in its journey for ages. This is the justification of life upon earth and its destiny and fulfillment. Such a spiritual life will harmonize the highest individualism with the greatest collective good, without either diminishing the other. Human progress is tending towards such a culmination.

The crisis we face today is essentially an evolutionary crisis. The solution is to be found in a conscious, collective effort towards evolution into a higher divine race. The Mother has made this clear in one of Her significant messages – "The future of the earth depends upon the change of consciousness. And the change is bound to come. But it is left up to men to decide whether they will collaborate for the change or the change will have to be enforced upon them by the power of crushing circumstances."

The question before us, therefore, is no more whether spiritual life is the only solution or not but rather whether or not we are ready for it. For, the spiritual man is bound to arise out of the mental man and replace him, just as man has replaced others before him. The choice before us is whether we consent to grow into the destined New Human Being or step aside and become extinct, paving the way for tomorrow's New Creation.

Madhu Tandan

AND ALL BEGINNINGS CEASE

Some years ago I had a dream which left a powerful impact on me: I'm sitting for an examination, and the invigilator hands me the question paper. I realize this is no ordinary examination, it is a life-exam. The first question is, "What is your gravest doubt in life?" I answer, "My doubt is that nothing is permanent. Everything changes. Today's pleasure is tomorrow's sorrow, despair turns to hope, health to illness, love to indifference. In this constant flux what is permanent?"

I continue to write in this vein for some time, and then feel that I need to get on to the next question, since time is running out. Even though I have not completed my answer, curiosity compels me to turn the page over and look at what the next question is. In rather bold letters it challenges me by asking: *Who are you?*

The dream was unexpected because I did not know what my gravest doubt was. Yet in the dream my answering the question in that manner seemed very normal. Then to be questioned, "Who are you," startled me, for the question was very similar to Ramana Maharishi's central teaching of "Who am I," which for him was the starting point of the inner enquiry. And how were the two questions related to each other?

In the days that followed, I was perplexed by the question of "Who am I." I soon realized how difficult the exercise was. No matter how much I thought about it, I was confronted by the mind's limitation to answer it. If I answered the question by "I'm a woman" or "I'm a working woman," or by even more abstract personal qualities whether good or bad, it did not answer the question. For I'm not just my gender nor my abilities, neither just my thoughts nor only my emotions. Even my personality traits are not me, nor am I just my ego – none of these were satisfactory answers to the question. Not individually, nor in their totality. I may think that all my personality traits, my thoughts and emotions make up the person I am, but that in essence is not "me." My thoughts and emotions constantly change, my body undergoes changes, my personality traits change, so how can I answer the question by attributes that fluctuate and alter?

I also began to see the connection between the first and second questions of my dream. If I realized the changing impermanence of human experience then the next question follows – "Is there anything permanent and unchanging?" And to find that out, "Who are you?" could become the starting point of my enquiry. The dream was highlighting an indication that doubts could lead to an inner enquiry.

This question of who I really was had perplexed me in another way when I was in my early twenties. I found, much to my surprise, many contradictory persons living under the same roof I called "me." A part of me liked company while another ran shy of it; one part wished to write and another found the mental discipline too strenuous to pursue. These contradictory pulls had no point of resolution, and I was carried forward by whatever was the slightly stronger desire of the moment. Living with these various selves was like sitting on an one-legged stool, and desiring stability. It just did not seem possible. Without realising it, I was seeking some fresh anchorage.

Initially, we are not sure whether there is anything to seek. It is our faith that beyond this everchanging flux of human experience there is something that endures. I felt there is something greater than myself that surrounds and affects me. My sensed connection with this power became the measure of my faith. Einstein had said, "Human beings, vegetables, or cosmic dust – we all dance to a mysterious tune, intoned in the distance by an invisible piper."

I couldn't take refuge in conventional religion, because Hinduism seemed to be operating from an antiquated past, while my convent education, woven with the religious doctrine of sin and guilt, had left me cold. Both had failed to provide the context to answer my questions, and it became difficult to place a living enquiry within their precincts. Mystical schools, with their direct approach, were more attractive.

Ramana Maharishi had said to Paul Brunton:

> Unless and until a man embarks on this quest of the true Self, doubt and uncertainty will follow his footsteps through life. The greatest kings and statesmen try to rule others when in their heart of hearts they know that they cannot rule themselves. Yet the greatest power is at the command of the man who has penetrated to his inmost depth ... What is the use of knowing about everything else when you do not yet know who you are? Men avoid this enquiry into their true Self, but what else is there so worthy to be undertaken?

Fired by faith and our heart's yearning that man's true purpose was to search for that which is highest in himself, my husband and I, both in our late twenties, left our comfortable life in Delhi to settle with our Teacher for seven years in his remote mountain abode.

My faith in my Teacher grew as he wove the inner and outer dimensions of my life into a harmoniously entwined thread: a way of living in which nothing was to be rejected, all of life was to be integrated as an offering to the inner enquiry. I was intrigued and inspired that such a vision was possible, and that a path led to it.

In the lifestyle he outlined, every experience would be part of the effort to produce wholeness: the body, the mind and the emotions, harnessed to serve a single intent – to "know thyself." I soon realized it was a "hands-on" search. Twelve hours of manual work each day would be offered in selfless service. This was intended to cut out the messy edges of gain and profit. The internal resistance to this strenuous work was to be tempered by introspection, while the complexities of our emotional nature would be understood by dream analysis. Meditation would help to stop the internal chatter of thoughts so as to reach the Self within. The attempt was to give recognition – through the body, mind and emotions – to that Higher Awareness.

In the years that followed I discovered how difficult it was to live by the belief of this Higher Awareness. We were being asked to think and act in consonance with this Awareness without knowing what it was! I had never experienced it, but I was living my days in the belief that it existed. All I had was faith in my Teacher's words. Plotinus says,

> This is not a journey for the feet; ever the feet bring us from one spot of earth to another. Nor do you need to plan a journey by horse-and-chariot or over sea. All this order of things you must set aside. Nor do you need to see; you must close the eyes and call upon another vision which is to be waked within you, a vision which all possess, which few apply.

This invocation to an intuited but yet unseen vision, is an act of faith. It is this very faith that helps one let go, slowly and painfully, of all that may obstruct one's vision of that Higher Reality. The vision of faith helps you let go without knowing what you are relinquishing it for. The goal ahead is shrouded in the mists of a mystery, while in the here-and-now the voice of my Teacher urged us to shed our excess emotional and mental baggage, so that the ascent to the snow-clad mountains is made unencumbered. But how was this to be done within the clamoring, overwhelming sound of our ambitions and aspirations?

Each mystical school has formulated its own methodology to find a way back to the Source. Though the practices differ, the essential stages in this journey are common.

It begins with an attempt to withdraw from the phenomenal world of sensory stimulus to an inner realm. Meditational exercises in the Hindu-Buddhistic tradition are such an attempt. Faith urges the seeker to look not towards the known, but to that which knows.

For any real knowledge rests only in the Knower. But the Knower is eclipsed by countless thoughts of our everyday concerns. In meditation the attempt is to find a silent and calm space within, which is free of all thoughts.

This is easier said than done. When I began to practise, I was appalled to see the number of thoughts which swarmed through my mind, akin to a beehive that has been disturbed. My thoughts were like yeast fermenting in the warm waters of desire, confronting me with repetitive regularity. How were they to be silenced? My teacher advised: "Don't use force by trying to subjugate them. Just watch them stream past you without identifying with any one of them. Observe them, watch their complex convolutions, their persistent attempts to attract your attention without passing judgment or getting swept away by them. Practise this again and again, and you will see how the inner silence will grow."

I learnt over time that thoughts do not stop. They are like hydra-headed monsters which, as soon as you slay one, spawns another. The only thing one could do would be to withdraw one's identification with them. The less I paid attention to the endless stream of thoughts, the less they bothered me. I also saw that if there was an angry thought persisting, by going over the thought, again and again, it ended in more anger, not less. Instead, if a real effort was made to watch the thoughts with detachment, as if viewing a play, they get to be seen for what they are — lifeless shells, floating down a stream.

There is a parable that the courtesan continues to dance as long as the Raja's attention stays upon her. As soon as his attention turns away, she stops dancing. It seemed the same with my thoughts. It was my interest and attention on them which powered them. If I could withdraw my attention, their compulsive dance would stop.

To silence the mind Hindus have the mantra, Muslims the name of Allah, Catholics their rosaries, Buddhists their prayer wheels, all of which become symbols of the transpersonal, acting as an anchor for the wandering mind. And every attempt is an effort to let go: to drop all those desires that are still warm from our chasing them; of our hopes still eager for their pursuit; of the taste, the scent and touch of a world that still fascinates us. Yet this shedding is done in faith. Faith in an unseen vision that beckons us with its promise of perfection. For finally, the attempt is to quieten the mind and find the Self – the essential I which can mirror the Highest within us. It is only a calm lake which will reflect the full splendor of the moon. T. S. Eliot is particularly compelling in his evocation of this in Burnt Norton:

At the still point of the turning world.
Neither flesh nor fleshless;
Neither from nor towards; at the still point, there the dance is,
But neither arrest nor movement.
And do not call it fixity,
Where past and future are gathered.
Neither movement from nor towards,
Neither ascent nor decline.
Except for the point,
the still point.

When finally one chances on the "still point" within, anyone who has attempted it will realize how much has been cast-off in meditation – so exhaustingly circular can the onslaught of thoughts be. The storm has raged, but a shelter has been found. Faith has found lodgings for the night, before the climb begins again in the morrow. This is not a state to be achieved once, but the seeker must be able to evoke it, time and again, till it burns like a steady inner flame. Eliot calls it the "still point," others have referred to it as the "calm witness" or the "watcher on the threshold," each marking a significant stage in the journey to that point where the cauldron of personality is no longer being stirred by the ladle of desires. All is deeply still, without a single wind stirring the mind.

Yet, this is not some rarefied state isolated from the process of everyday living. In fact the ability to contact the "still point" can have a profound effect on the life we live. The calm certainty contacted within is likely to spill over into our day. If the twisting arteries of our thoughts and emotions are viewed from the stable reference of the "witness," many of the confusions and uncertainties we face may find a new vantage point of dispassion. The very faith that helped us let go of our thoughts in meditation will strengthen the process of outer clarity.

The all-important transition will have been made from *person* to the *witness*, in the terminology used by the modern mystic, Nisargadatta Maharaj. The disciple may feel that the back of the struggle has been broken, and only the last steady incline has to be traversed. But no, there still remains, a final letting go if the answer to "Who am I?" is to be attained. The *Lankavatara Sutra* talks about "the turning around in the deepest seat of consciousness." And about this leg of the journey, Plotinus says:

> To attain it is for those that are willing to take the upward way, for those that will turn away from other things for it, divest themselves of all we have gathered round us by our descent. So to those that go up to the holy celebrations of the Mysteries there are appointed purifications and the laying aside of the garments worn before and the approach in nakedness ...

The Sufis speak of "seeking to be drowned" (*istighraq*), of *fana al-fana* or extinction in the Eternal.

Until now anything that impeded the ascent of the aspirant had to be dropped, but now *all* experience – not only thoughts and memories but the identification with the body, everything that feeds the illusion of separateness – has to be exhausted. There is no distinction of any kind. All is One. There is no one to know and nothing to be known. No this, no that; no here, no there; no now, no then. Only a state of utter, incandescent unity. This is the *Nirvana* of the Buddhists, the *Parabrahman* of the Hindus; the *al-Haqq* of the Sufis; the Holy Grail of the Chivalric tradition, or the Philosopher's Stone of the Alchemists.

The stage of the "calm witness" or "still point" has been left behind in the foothills of the climb. It had been but a foothold the pilgrim once used in his courageous ascent. For now the traveller is no longer a seeker, but one who has found. The disciple's faith has been honored. What once was faith has now become certainty.

What can be said after this, except that one's head bows at such an achievement. There are probably many seekers who make the inward attempt, but rare are those who make it to the summit.

And those that do have been moved by a faith, and an awesome intent to drop everything that obscured their vision of the Absolute.

Nature's cycle of the seed, the stalk, the bud and the flower could describe this search in which at every stage faith is the charge that helps the seeker to let go of something, and thereby step onto the next rung of the ladder. When the seed of enquiry is sown in the ground, the outer has to be relinquished in an attempt to turn inwards. The inward stalk can only grow if the weeds of thoughts do not suffocate it. Thoughts have to be let go of so that the bud of stillness finds its home. Finally even the bud of stillness has to be left behind for the Bliss of the Absolute. The promise of the seed must fulfill itself in the flowering tree.

Faith is an act of courage. For it is prepared to believe and follow something essentially unseen, driven by a vision which has no tangible proof. Yet, it trusts its heart's yearnings and sets off on an untrodden mountain track in search of some inviolate sanctuary, which few have seen. That faith is tested again and again, because at every point a barrier appears which can only be crossed if something is given up. Slowly and painfully the seeker divests himself of his luggage, not knowing how far his lodgings are. In the evening hour doubts creep into his heart as he wonders if his search is just a myth. Faith then becomes an exacting master who claims the surrender of those doubts, lest they become an excuse from the demands of renewed effort.

He who taught dependent arising
As unceasing, unborn
Not broken, not permanent,
Not coming, not going.
Not with separate nature, not with one nature,
In peace, without manifestation,
To him the accomplished Buddha
The supreme teacher I bow down.
Nagarjuna

Legend has it that the painted images of the Buddha had originated in central India, now geographically located in the state of Bihar. The principal school of art from which Tibetan painting has been derived dates back to the eighth century. It was followed by a celebration of spiritual rebirth in an explosion of creative outpouring from Tibetan artists and scholars. We witness the unique and breath-taking character of Tibetan arts and spirituality in the Thangka paintings.

The creation of a Thangka scroll, however, is not just another style of painting. It has great religious significance. It transcends the terrain of line and color and gently takes the mind to the realm of spirituality where the practitioner becomes one with the deity depicted on the canvas. The paintings are commissioned for varied benedictions. The primary intent is to create an object of worship that will help to gather merit in this life. But Thangkas are also made to seek practical help: in sickness, for bringing about prosperity, for protection from impending danger, and to assist in the rebirth of a recently departed person. Devotion is the shared realm for both artist and practitioner, and this coupled with meticulous care and precision gives the Thangka its unique character and divinity. The details are worked upon meditatively so as to earn the karma required to gain freedom from samsara.

Finally, if the painting is to function as a sacred object it is mounted on a brocade frame and then consecrated through a number of rituals: combining meditation, incantation and recitation of mantras; the back of the painting is inscribed with the three syllables that indicate the body, speech and mind of the main figure.

Peter Tyler

THE NEXT CERTITUDE

> I look back on the stretch of past years and see the
> crumbling ruins of a proud civilization lying heaped as
> garbage out of history! And yet I shall not commit the
> grievous sin of losing faith in Man, accepting his present
> defeat as final. I shall look forward to a turning in history
> after the cataclysm is over and the sky is again unburdened
> and passionless.
>
> Perhaps the new dawn will come from this horizon, from
> the East where the sun rises; and then, unvanquished Man
> will retrace his path of conquest, despite all barriers, to
> win back his lost heritage.

So spoke Nobel Laureate Rabindranath Tagore in his last address "Crisis in Civilization," published in the dark year of 1941.[1] As we approach the end of what in Europe is termed "The Second Millennium" and stand on the threshold of what does in fact appear to be a new era it is hard not to feel with the old poet that the twentieth century has witnessed "the crumbling ruins of a proud civilization" as Europe, that great defender of "civilized values," descended during this century to its darkest and most barbaric level.

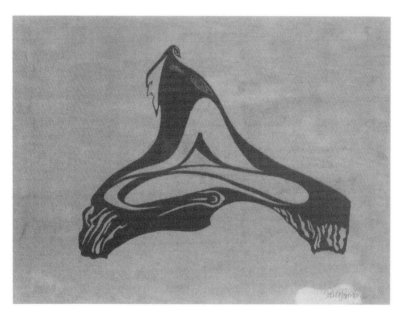

RABINDRANATH TAGORE
NAMAZ
ink on paper
Courtesy: National Gallery of Modern Art, New Delhi.

Writing in 1992, the philosopher Isaiah Berlin stated:

> I have lived through most of the twentieth century without, I must add, suffering personal hardship. I remember it only as the most terrible century in Western history.[2]

Yet, despite all the terrible things we have witnessed this century, like Tagore we somehow feel we cannot give up hope. We do look forward to a "turning in history" when the cataclysm is over.

Tagore suggested in 1941 that perhaps the "new dawn" would come from "this horizon, from the East where the sun rises." How prescient of him to see that! Just two decades later all the youth of the West (led famously by "The Beatles") were trekking to India to "seek enlightenment." The pilgrimage continues till today – perhaps somewhat more balanced and realistic than in the heady days of the sixties, but unabated.

Yet as the western world ends its "short and terrible" twentieth century there is no doubt that the West has an uneasy sense that in all its technological advances it has lost something. The West (and by this phrase I do not just mean the geographical west, but all those that benefit from the massive technological advances of the past-half century) enjoys a standard of living the like of which has probably never before been experienced, yet it knows it is not happy – it is uneasy and uncertain and is staggering into the uncertainty of the future looking perhaps for that "new dawn from the East" which Tagore spoke of.

The Search for Spirituality

The struggle seeking a new identity is often couched in terms of the "search for spirituality." This is usually described in grand, sweeping and slightly unfocused terms. In *The Politics of Spirituality*, William Stringfellow writes:

> "Spirituality" may indicate stoic attitudes, occult phenomena, the practice of so-called mind control, yoga discipline, escapist fantasies, interior journeys, an appreciation of Eastern religions, multifarious pious exercises, superstitious imaginations, intensive journals, dynamic muscle tension,

assorted dietary regimes, meditation, jogging, cults, monastic rigors, mortification of the flesh, wilderness sojourns, political resistance, contemplation, abstinence, hospitality, a vocation of poverty, non-violence, silence, the efforts of prayer, obedience, generosity, exhibiting stigmata, entering solitude ...

And the movement that has coalesced in the West around this search has at some time or other incorporated one or other of the above (look at the diverse contents of the world bestseller *The Little Book of Calm* for evidence of this).

How Can We Make Sense of This?

Turning once again to Tagore we find in his life and writings a sort of presentiment of this search for a "spirituality beyond religion" that is so characteristic of our times. When once asked "What is your religion?" he wrote:

What is generally called "religion," I cannot say I have achieved within myself in a clear deep-rooted form. But there has been in my mind a steady onward growth of something alive which I have felt on many an occasion. It is not, by any means, a particular conception – but a deep awareness, a new awakening. I can see so well that I shall gradually be able to come to terms with myself; that mingling my sorrows and joys, the within and without, my conduct and belief, I shall be able to give to my life a sense of wholeness ... This never-dying mysterious relationship that exists between me and this infinite universe-life has a language – knowable and strangely manifest through the melody of color and smell.[3]

Further, that this creative force:

the force that has given one whole significance to all the joys, sorrows and incidents of my life, the force that is threading my death and various births into one continuity, and through which I feel the unity with the created universe of all animate and inanimate objects, I have described as "God of Life."

Two consequences can be derived from this position – first that we are impelled to move towards greater integration and wholeness, and secondly, that this integration will be accompanied by increasing and inflaming love. We shall now turn to the implications of these two positions.

The Need for Integration

As human beings we long for integration, it is our fundamental need. As such I see the new and radical search for spirituality that is characteristic of our time as being clearly marked by this search for integration.

This integration appears to be happening on three levels and we shall consider each in turn.

1. INTRAPERSONAL INTEGRATION: One clear characteristic of the "New Spirituality" is its desire to take in the whole person. No longer can spirituality be seen as something that is practised by remote and divorced yogis who have no connection with everyday life. In the West there is a flight of people from churches and religious institutions that has been described as "not so much bleeding as haemorrhaging."

Thus the new spirituality encourages greater body integration: the use of yoga and body posture, the incorporation of breath and *chakra* concentration. Commonplace, perhaps, in the East, but often unheard of and perhaps a little mistrusted in the West.

There is a greater acceptance of sexuality and a desire to reclaim the sexual in the western tradition, especially in Christianity. Contemporary writers such as Matthew Fox draw our attention to the use made of the Hebrew *Song of Songs* by the medieval Christian writers – a collection of passionate erotic hymns to the divine as beautiful and inspired as the songs of Mirabai or the *Gita Govinda.*

Finally, the twentieth century insights of psychology are beginning to be taken seriously by this spirituality. No longer are Freud and Jung disparaged but seen as advocates of a method that allows greater insight and wisdom into the workings of the human mind and its integration into the whole person. This has, interestingly enough, been accompanied by a greater awareness amongst therapists and psychologists of the role that spirituality plays in psychic healing and the need to take it seriously in a clinical setting.

2. INTERPERSONAL INTEGRATION: Just as there is a felt need for intrapersonal integration, so the new spirituality takes the relations between people equally seriously. Never before has there been such a pressing need for equality and justice in the world. The hallmarks of any authentic spirituality has been its ability to bring its followers an increased sense of responsibility for the well-being of those around them. So we find an increased importance attached to the need for help for the economically or socially disadvantaged. The importance of empowering the marginalized and oppressed – whether on grounds of gender, race, sexuality, disability, ethnicity or any other.

Both Western and Eastern writers and practitioners of spirituality in the twentieth century have carried this characteristic. Sri Aurobindo, Mother Teresa, Martin Luther King and Mahatma Gandhi, all come to mind. The passionate struggle for social justice is not divorced from the spiritual search but intimately connected with it.

3. TRANSPERSONAL INTEGRATION: The final element of the new spirituality is a need for integration between the individual and the cosmos.

As we end a century which has seen unprecedented damage done to the environment and the ecosystem by the blindness and greed of humanity there is a growing awareness that we belong to a finely tuned global system which once destroyed is destroyed forever.

The depletion of the ozone layer, global warming, the pollution of our rivers and seas and nuclear catastrophes such as Chernobyl have been as wake-up calls to a sleeping ecological conscience in humanity.

The New Spirituality is marked by its eco-awareness and the need for respect in our treatment of the earth and its denizens.

Conclusions

I have described here in brief and general terms what I see as the essential characteristics of the New Spirituality that is emerging from the ashes of the twentieth century. We live in a time of rapid and unprecedented change and the next fifty years shall surely see advances as great, if not greater, as those of the past fifty. Like Tagore, we can perhaps step into the uncertainty of that future with a confidence that the spirituality and love innate in humanity will reassert itself. A hope never better expressed than in these lines from Tagore's *Gitanjali*:

> Have you not heard his silent steps? He comes, comes, ever comes.
>
> Every moment and every age, every day and every night he comes, comes, ever comes.
>
> Many a song have I sung in many a mood of mind, but all their notes have always proclaimed, "He comes, comes, ever comes."
>
> In the fragrant days of April through the forest path he comes, comes, ever comes.
>
> In the rainy gloom of July nights on the thundering chariot of clouds he comes, comes, ever comes.
>
> In sorrow after sorrow it is his steps that press upon my heart, and it is the golden touch of his feet that makes my joy to shine.[4]

Notes

1. From *Crisis in Civilisation* reprinted in *Towards Universal Man*, Asia Publishing House, Visva-Bharati, Santiniketan, p. 359.
2. Quoted in E. Hobsbawm, *Age of Extremes: The Short Twentieth Century*, London: Michael Joseph, 1994, p. 1.
3. Quoted in "Tagore, Reconciler of East and West" by Mulk Raj Anand in *Rabindranath Tagore: A Biography of his Visions and Ideas*, ed. V. Grover. *Ideas*, Deep and Deep, New Delhi, 1998.
4. Reprinted in *Collected Poems and Plays of Rabindranath Tagore*, Delhi: Macmillan, 1982, p. 21.

Marcus Braybrooke

FROM FAIR WORDS TO SHARED EXPERIENCE

Religion in some societies has almost become synonymous with extremism and communalism. It is seen as a cause of division and even of death. In Northern Ireland, a fourteen year old Protestant, when her father was shot dead, said, "I am ashamed of my religion." He was the only Protestant among seven victims, the rest were Catholic. Two Protestant gunmen had sprayed customers of a bar with automatic gunfire in "revenge" for the murder of Protestants by Catholics during the previous week.

Not long after that tragedy, came a newspaper headline, "The little Bosnian girl whose mistake was to be a Muslim." These stories could be paralleled from Sri Lanka or the Middle East or any other part of the world. Disillusionment with all religions would be an understandable reaction. Yet, for all the cruelty and obscurantism associated with religion, hidden within the great traditions of faith are precious resources for the future welfare of humanity and these are too important to be abandoned to the extremists.

The interfaith movement is a sign of hope for the world and for restoring credibility to religion itself. Ironically, some of the strongest opponents of attempts to develop understanding and cooperation between the world's religions, are members of these religions. Paradoxically, the search for unity has itself been divisive. Indeed it is sometimes said that if you make friends with people of other religions, you will make enemies of some members of your own.

The Interfaith Movement

The last twenty-five years have seen great efforts to replace the traditional hostility between religions with a new spirit of fellowship and dialogue. The beginning of the interfaith movement dates back to the World's Parliament of Religions held in Chicago in 1893, attended by Swami Vivekananda, Dharmapala and many other distinguished religious leaders. Efforts to carry on the spirit of the Parliament were made by the International Association for Religious Freedom and the World Congress of Faiths. Mahatma Gandhi was also an early advocate of interfaith fellowship. Throughout this century there has been a considerable growth in the scholarly study of religions and in publications about the world religions.

Even so, the real development of interfaith work had to wait until the last quarter of this century. It was in 1968 that the first Spiritual Summit Conference, arranged by the Temple of Understanding, was held in Calcutta, and the first Assembly of the World Conference on Religion and Peace met in Kyoto, Japan in 1970. Five years earlier, the Second Vatican Council of the Roman Catholic Church had agreed on the historic document, *Nostra Aetate*, which marked a new and more sympathetic attitude to the other religions of the world. The Decree stressed what human beings have in common, and recognized that "there has existed among diverse peoples a certain perception of that hidden power which hovers over the course of things."[1] Reference was made to the contemplation of the divine mystery in Hinduism and to Buddhism's recognition of the "radical insufficiency of this shifting world."[2] At the same time, the Vatican established a secretariat for non-Christians which was renamed the Pontifical Council for Inter-religious Dialogue in 1989. In 1971, the World Council of Churches, which brings together Protestant and Orthodox churches, set up a Sub-Unit on Dialogue between People of Living Faiths and Ideologies headed by the distinguished Indian scholar, Stanley Samartha.

The desire of a growing number of Christians to replace mission by dialogue was reciprocated by many members of other faiths. Gradually, the circle of interfaith dialogue grew and in 1993 – the centenary year of the first World's Parliament of Religions – major interfaith gatherings were held at Bangalore, in Japan and above all at Chicago. Since the 1993 Parliament of Religions, activity has continued to increase and an International Interfaith Center has been established at Oxford to help coordinate worldwide interfaith work and to promote research to find ways to make this most effective.[3]

Common Action for a World in Need

Many people hope that religions can act together for a better world. Indeed, Charles Bonney, who was president of the 1893 Parliament, said, "When the religious faiths of the world recognize each other as brothers, children of the one Father, whom all profess to love and serve, then, and not till then, will the nations of the earth yield to the Spirit of concord and learn to war no more."[4]

It is recognized that religion is often a cause of communalism and conflict. In many situations, as already mentioned, religious differences add bitterness to the hostility. It is hoped that by dispelling ignorance and prejudice and by encouraging people of different faith communities to meet, this bitterness can be purged and indeed that people from different faiths can become agents of reconciliation. This, however, can be unpopular with one's own faith community. If members of other religions are seen as "the enemy," then even talking to them can be risky and be seen as betrayal. Those Jews and Muslims in the Middle East who were the first to be prepared to meet each other and to begin to build bridges of friendship often had to do so secretly. The same was true of Protestants and Catholics in Northern Ireland who opened up the way to reconciliation. One Buddhist monk in Sri Lanka has told how he went to live in the Tamil Hindu city of Jaffna and as a sign of peace just walked around smiling at people. It was nearly ten months before anyone smiled back!

Christians too who have adopted the way of dialogue have been accused of "betraying" Jesus Christ by other Christians who hold that as he is the Savior of the world, a Christian's calling is to try to convert others to have faith in him.

Despite the opposition from within, the number of people enriched by friendships with members of other faith communities has steadily increased. As this continued to happen, they felt a growing desire to act together for peace and for the relief of suffering, and to affirm the values which people of different religions hold in common. The concern came to a head at the 1993 Parliament in Chicago. The Assembly of Religious and Spiritual Leaders devoted their time to discussing "A Declaration Toward a Global Ethic." It began with the statement:

> The world is in agony ... Peace eludes us ... the planet is being destroyed ... neighbors live in fear... women and men are estranged from each other ... children die.[5]

It is widely recongized that the great crises that confront the world today – the poverty, the violence, the damage to the environment – are at root spiritual and ethical. There are, for example, enough resources to feed the world's peoples but there is no will to share them. The Declaration, however, did offer a message of hope. It affirmed that there was sufficient agreement between the religions on how we should live and there could be a fundamental change in our situation if we followed that teaching:

> The basis for an ethic already exists. This ethic offers the possibility of a better individual and global order, and leads individuals away from despair and societies away from chaos.

The basic ethical principle is:

> ... that every human being must be treated humanely. This means that every human being without distinction of age, sex, race, skin, color, physical or mental ability, language, religion, political view, or national or social origin possesses an inalienable and untouchable dignity.

From this follow four commitments: (i) To a culture of non-violence and respect for life, (ii) To a culture of solidarity and a just economic order, (iii) To a culture of tolerance and a life of truthfulness, and (iv) To a culture of equal rights and partnership between men and women.

Whilst the Declaration affirms that "a common set cf core values is found in the teachings of the religions, and these form the basis of a global ethic," not all members of religions agree with this affirmation. There are those who would question whether ethical teaching can be separated from the whole structure of a religion's belief. Others ask "Are the agreements more apparent than real?" or "Is the document an attempt to impose Western cultural values on the rest of the world?" There are valid criticisms, both of the procedure by which the ethic was drawn up and of its methodology and content. Yet some of the criticisms seem to be an attempt to hide the fact that many religious communities do not themselves live up to the four commitments. It is clear that some religious people are not wholly committed to non-violence and would accept the use of force to defend victims of aggression. At the Parliament itself, there was debate about what this phrase meant. In its early years, when the World Conference of Religion and Peace focused on the need for nuclear disarmament, not all religious communities identified with this. Again, few religious communities really practise "a culture of equal rights and partnership between men and women."

Advocates of the Declaration thus become critics of their own faith community. A commitment to human rights and an active concern to safeguard the environment are evident at many interfaith gatherings – more so, it seems to me, than at gatherings of the faithful. Those members of a religious tradition who play an active part in interfaith organizations are likely therefore to be identified with socially radical policies and to be critical of their own tradition.

Comparatively Religious

The most insidious threat from the interfaith movement in the eyes of traditionalists is to the truth claims of its faith community. There is an old quip that the person who studies comparative religion ends up "comparatively religious." Obviously, this threat is felt more acutely in faith traditions which stress correct belief, whereas in India, it is often said that all religions are paths up the same mountain.

Religions of revelation are likely to emphasize the intellectual content of belief. Let me illustrate this from the religion to which I belong – Christianity. It used to be the custom in the Church of England on certain occasions to say the so-called Athanasian creed. It begins like this:

> Whosoever will be saved: before all things it is necessary that he hold the Catholic Faith.
> Which Faith except every one do keep whole and undefiled: without doubt he shall perish everlastingly.[6]

The assumption was that salvation depended on correct belief. At one time, those who denied this were burnt as heretics. The Bible was assumed to have been dictated by God and every word was correct. The major shift is that many, like the great Archbishop William Temple, now see that Revelation is, in its fullest sense, the revelation of the very being of God, to which the Bible points. Living experience of God is primary, scripture and doctrine is secondary.

This emphasis on religious experience – one might call it a mystical approach – opens the way for appreciation of other faith traditions. The symbols, the scriptures and the teachings may be very different, but do they perhaps point beyond themselves to a common experience of the Divine?[7]

This is not the place to enter into theological and philosophical discussion of these issues. For many of those in the interfaith movement, it is the actual meeting with people of other faiths and attending their places of worship which has convinced them that others also have a genuine knowledge of the Divine. I recall a long drive in South India. At one point the driver turned to me and said "You are a Christian, my friend is a Hindu and I am a Muslim – but we all worship One God."

It is this that those who claim exclusive possession of the truth find so objectionable and it is a view strongly resisted by all so-called religious fundamentalists. It is, I think, important to distinguish traditionalists from fundamentalists. Traditionalists may never have questioned the truth of their religion. Fundamentalists, as Martin Marthy has argued, are essentially oppositional and reject new ways of thinking about religion.[8] They adopt an a-historical attitude to the central truths of their religion as being unchanging and not open to reinterpretation in a changing world. They reject historical criticism of their scriptures. They also reject the idea of symbolism, taking their particular myths as true in a literal sense. This implies that other religions are false.

Fundamentalists also, I think, reject or are unaware of changes in our understanding of the nature of human knowledge. As Leonard Swidler has explained in his *The Meaning of Life at the Edge of the Third Millennium*, our understanding of truth statements has been "de-absolutized." We recognize that all statements about reality are conditioned by their author's historical setting, intention, culture, class and sex. Further we recognize the limits of language and that all knowledge is interpreted knowledge. Reality speaks to each person with the language he or she gives to it. We are not in a position to make ultimate, unconditional statements. Language about Ultimate Reality is symbolic and poetic.[9]

There is, therefore, a profound struggle within many religious communities between the fundamentalists, who will claim to be defenders of the true faith, and the more mystical who recognize with Paul Tillich that "in the depth of every living religion there is a point at which religion itself loses its importance, and that to which it points breaks through its particularity, elevating it to spiritual freedom and to a vision of the spiritual presence in other expressions of the ultimate meaning of man's existence."[10]

Why Bother with Religion?

There are many who now question the role of institutional religion. The situation of course varies in different countries and with different religions. In Europe and much of North America there is a decline in church and synagogue membership. It is still too early to judge whether Hindus and Sikhs and Muslims born in the West will remain active members of their respective faith communities, but the influence of secularism seems to be all pervasive.

But there is a deeper question about the role of the religious community. Many who are disillusioned with religion are people of deep spiritual sensitivity. As long ago as 1970, Jacob Needleman wrote that "the contemporary disillusionment with religion has revealed itself to be a *religious disillusionment*.[11] Are traditional religions the setting for spiritual growth or only a way by which a group of people seek to preserve their identity and influence? In every age the mystic has had an uneasy relationship with "official" religion.

As traditional community links grow weaker, at least in the West, religion becomes more of an individual path and there will be those who in their spiritual search draw inspiration from many of the great faiths of the world. There has also been a considerable growth of new spiritual movements and many in the West have turned for inspiration to teachers from India. Significantly, the newer spiritual movements, which perhaps eschew any doctrinal teaching and emphasize meditation and spiritual knowledge, do play a role, disproportionate to their size, at interfaith gatherings. This too can increase the suspicions of traditionalists.

During most of my involvement in national and international interfaith activity, I have also been a parish priest. For me being rooted in a faith community has given me strength for a wider concern. Those who know their own identity and are confident in their own faith, will not feel threatened by the faith of others. Indeed because they treasure their own, they will respect the faith of others and seek to learn from it.

John S. Dunne in his book *The Way of All the Earth*, had spoken of "passing over."

> Passing over from one culture to another, from one way of life to another, from one religion to another ... It is followed by an equal and opposite process we might call "coming back," coming back with new insight to one's own culture, one's own way of life, one's own religion. The holy man of our time, it seems, is not a figure like Gotama or Jesus or Mohammad, a man who could found

a world religion, but a figure like Gandhi, a man who passes over by sympathetic understanding from his own religion to other religions and comes back with new insight to his own.[12]

This is my own experience and I believe it can be a way forward for the religious life of the world. I have been shaped by my experience of God's love in Jesus Christ, but through my contacts with people of other faiths and the wisdom of other religions, my own faith has been deepened and broadened. Questions of ritual and even of doctrine have seemed less important, whereas the conviction of God's universal love and the sanctity of every human being has become more compelling. In the same way, even as religious communities encounter each other in a spirit of dialogue, they are coming to see that there are many ways of worshipping the Divine Reality and many ways of speaking of the Divine Mystery, but that the essential attributes of that Divine Reality are emphasized in all traditions. I recall attending a Sikh conference in Delhi and almost every speaker emphasized the love of God. If I had shut my eyes, I could have imagined that I was at a Christian conference. Visiting Tibet, I came to see how Compassion is central to that tradition of Buddhism. The Sufi mystics and the Tamil Saivite poets speak with passion of the love of God.

We have hardly begun to explore the depths of each other's spiritual traditions. Much interfaith activity has been either intellectual discussion or practical efforts for peace and human welfare. As we meet "in the cave of the heart," we discover a Divine Presence which transcends all our tradition but which encompasses us all in love.

It is this rich spiritual resource that the world needs and this is why religious extremists and fundamentalists cannot be allowed to become the guardians of the world's great religious traditions. The interfaith movement can help to ensure that these spiritual treasures are available for all people as they struggle to build a world society of peace, justice and compassion, where every life is valued and the earth itself is treated with reverence.

Notes

1. Nostra Aetate, "Declaration on the Relationship of the Church to Non-Christian Religions" in *The Documents of Vatican II*, ed. W. M. Abbott SJ, Geoffrey Chapman, 1966, p. 661.
2. Ibid, p. 662.
3. The Chicago Parliament has established a continuing body known as The Council for a Parliament of the World's Religions. A United Religions Initiative and an International Peace Council have also been established. See further my *Faith and Interfaith in a Global Age*, CoNexus Press and Braybrooke Press, 1998.
4. *The World's Parliament of Religions*, ed. John Henry Barrows, Chicago, 1893, p. 67.
5. Quotations are from the Introduction of "Toward A Declaration of A Global Ethic," in *A Global Ethic*, SCM Press 1993, pp. 13-6.
6. *Quiqunque Vult*, verses 1-2.
7. See the first chapter of my *Explorer's Guide to Christianity*, Hodder and Stoughton, 1998 and *Spiritual Experience That Crosses Religious Divisions*, Religious Experience Research Centre, Westminster College, Oxford, 1999.
8. M. E. Marty, "What is Fundamentalism?" in *Fundamentalism As an Ecumenical Challenge*, Concilium Special, SCM Press, 1992.
9. Leonard Swidler, *The Meaning of Life at the Edge of the Third Millennium*, Paulist Press, 1992.
10. Paul Tillich, *Christianity and the Encounter of World Religions*, Columbia University Press, 1963, p. 97.
11. Jacob Needleman, *The New Religions*, Penguin, 1972, p. xi.
12. John S. Dunne, *The Way of All the Earth*, Macmillan, New York, 1972; SPCK, London, 1973, p. vii.

Maulana Wahiduddin

AFFIRMATION OF LIFE

What is spirituality? To use the Quranic term, *rabbaniyat*, it is the elevation of the human condition to a plane on which the mind is focused on the higher, non-material realities of a godly existence. The opposite of spirituality is materialism, a course followed all too often in this world. One who takes this course, giving all his attention to worldly things, or to put it another way, who centers his attention on mere appearances, is regarded as being materialistic-minded. Conversely, one who rises above material things or appearances, and finds his focus of interest in non-material things, is regarded as being spiritual or godly. The latter is one who obeys the injunction of the *Quran*: "Be devoted servants of God" (3:79) or, alternatively, "O people, be godly servants of Allah."

To understand what constitutes materialism, imagine that you come across a palatial house, or see an attractive car being driven along the street. If a strong desire is kindled within you to possess these things, it is a clear indication that materialism is a major motivating factor in your life. One who sees the same things but remains unaffected by the notions of luxury that they convey, and therefore feels no desire to acquire them, lives in a more rarefied sphere in which materialism plays no part. He feels no attraction to the lesser world of material appearances, for his soul resides on the profound level of spirituality.*

This is the truth, without any exaggeration. Those who live for worldly pleasures believe that gratification can be had only from material things. Worldly pleasure being the only thing they have experienced, they imagine they must depend solely on it. This thinking, however, comes from sheer ignorance. Had they experienced spiritual pleasure they would certainly have ignored the worldly ones. The pleasure derived from material things is limited in nature and very short-lived, whereas spiritual pleasure is lasting and may be savored eternally.

Tasty food, for instance, gives us a sense of enjoyment. But it is only when the experience of eating leads on to an outpouring of thanks-giving to God that our pleasure knows no bounds. Riding in a modern car is also very enjoyable, but that pleasure which comes from a deeper perception of reality and the appreciation of God's indescribably unique power – manifested in the world and the things created for man's comfort, including cars, aeroplanes and modern amenities – is a pleasure far superior to that of travelling in a luxurious automobile.

The materially minded find pleasure only in the things which they experience individually, but the spiritual person lives on a higher plane, and even seeing things in another's possession calls forth an outpouring of gratefulness to God from the innermost depths of the heart. The pleasure of the other person transforms itself into a spiritual pleasure for himself. A materially minded person sees only the creature, while a spiritually inclined person sees the splendor of the Creator through the creature. The spiritual riches accruing from the discovery of the Creator cannot be gained only through the discovery of the objects of creation.

Furthermore, in the spiritual world the difference between comfort and deprivation is not of great importance. The experience brought by material gains and its pleasures is of little value compared to what one gains from the experience of deprivation. Tears of pain from an aching heart bring as great a

* *The Koran*, translated by M. H. Shakir, Goodword Books, New Delhi, 1999.

relief as the laughter of happiness, for the very source of pleasure is in the remembrance of God. It is this reality which is expressed in a verse of the *Quran*: "It is only in the remembrance of God that hearts are comforted" (13:28). Comfort here means not just the temporary solace to be found in everyday convenience, but real and lasting comfort. For the materialist there is the pleasure of laughter, in spirituality there is pleasure within pain. Materialism lives a life of limitations, spirituality lives in the limitless.

Source of Divine Inspiration

The universe has been so fashioned by God that it may be a source of spiritual inspiration for man. According to the *Quran*, it is the quality of *tawassum* (15:75) that enables one to find inspiration in the universe. *Tawassum* (from *mutawassimin*) is the ability to understand the portent signs of nature, that is, to observe the phenomena of the universe in order to learn lessons from them and draw spiritual nourishment from events in the physical world.

Tawassum is, in a sense, a matter of conversion – as when grass enters the body of the cow and through a natural process is transformed into milk. Similarly, the truly religious person is like a divine industry. He is able to convert his observation of physical events into spiritual experience. He extracts spiritual nourishment from material things.

The distinguishing characteristic of wise people described in the *Quran* is that they continuously draw such sustenance from their environment, thus maintaining their intellectual and spiritual well-being. The *Quran* says,

> In the creation of the heavens and the earth, and in the succession of night and day, there are signs for men of understanding; those that remember God when standing, sitting, and lying down, and reflect on the creation of the heavens and the earth (saying): "Lord, you have not created these in vain, Glory be to You! Save us from the torment of the fire, Lord." (3:191)

A Personal Experience

It was morning on Thursday, 17 June, 1999. I was in Manchester,

staying in the house of an Arab brother, Dr. Arif. Sitting in my
room upstairs, I heard a gentle knock on the door. When I opened
it, I found a child of about five years of age. It was Qanita, the
first-born daughter of Dr. Arif. She said, all innocence and
gentleness, "Do you need anything?" (*turidu haja*). Perhaps it was
her mother who had sent her. It was a simple question. But I was
so overwhelmed by the innocent voice that I could utter no word
in reply. This normal incident became transformed in my mind
into an extraordinary event. *Turidu haja?* I felt as if God had sent
this little angel to ask after me and provide for my needs. "Do
you need anything?" The sunshine was on the flowers outside and
the birds were chirping on the trees, as if repeating the same words
to fill the universe.

A famous *hadith* came to mind: "Your Lord descends to this
worldly haven every day, looks at His servants and says, *Is there
anyone who has a need and asks Me, that I may give it to him?*"

For a while, I felt that I could see the whole universe on the
screen of my mind. It was a spiritual experience which could not
be expressed in language. It began as though God, through a little
girl, was saying, to me, "O My servant, do you need anything?"
and then, it extended to include the whole universe with its heavens
and its earth.

The vast heaven was asking, "Do you need a shelter? Here I
am to provide you with one, because God has ordered me to
do so." The gleaming sun was saying, "Do you need light? I am
here to supply it and transform your darkness into light." The
majestic mountain was announcing, "Would you like to climb to
the highest peak of humanity? Here I am to help you attain it."
The flowing waters of the river were murmuring, "Do you want
to have a spiritual bath to purify your soul? I am here to offer
you that." And the wind was asking, "Do you want to tour the
universe to see the wondrous signs of God? Here is my back
for you to ride on for such a divine journey." The trees were
whispering, "Would you like to become as radiant as we are? We
are here to make your wish come true." The fruits on their
branches and the crops in their husks were declaring, "If you

crave nourishment for your intellectual and spiritual life, we are here to provide you with it."

I heard in my mind these words: "O servant of God! Here is good news for you: If you have a need, then God has made the whole universe to serve your needs. God is so generous that He has created the whole of the universe to be at your service, day and night. In addition to this, if you show thankfulness to God, He will give you what is greater than all of this – Eternal Paradise in which there will be ... neither fear nor grievance." And then, "... He gave you all that you asked for." Whatever man needs to live a good life on this earth has been prepared in advance by God, directly and indirectly. Horses, for instance, were directly created; whereas aeroplanes were provided indirectly. The voice travelling through the air is an example of direct provision, while its transmission by means of electronic equipment is a form of indirect provision. Perhaps, this is what is meant by the following Quranic verse: "And (He has created) horses, mules and donkeys for you to ride, and as an adornment. And He has created (other) things which are beyond your knowledge" (*Quran* 16.8).

God Almighty says:

O you who believe!
Eat of the good things
That We have provided for you.
And be grateful to Allah,
If it is Him you worship.

Quran 2:172

This means that God Almighty has created everything imaginable and unimaginable, great and small, in the most perfect form. Then, He gave all this free to Man. The only price to be paid for these endless blessings is thankfulness; it is Man's recognition, from the depths of his heart, that God is the Giver and Man is the receiver.

Affirmation of Life

God revealed himself in the two books – the *Quran* and the Universe. The *Quran* is a literal version of God's word, while the

Universe, or Nature, is a practical elucidation of it. These two are the basic sources of spiritual inspiration for a man who seeks to live a life according to the divine scheme.

This dual source of divine inspiration the *Quran* describes thus:

> "God is He who raised the Heavens without visible supports, then He ascended the Throne. He has compelled the sun and the moon to be of service, each pursuing an appointed course; He controls the affairs (of the Universe); He makes plain His revelations, so that you may be certain of the meeting with your Lord. (13:2)

So, a *mumin* (true believer) has that kind of a prepared mind which, on seeing the Universe with its parts functioning in absolute coherence, exclaims, "There is no god but the one God!" and when he examines it, finds that despite so many complex happenings in its vastness, the Universe is highly predictable. With this discovery, he has a sense of God suggesting that he himself should have a predictable character, and just as the diverse parts of the Universe function in absolute harmony, in like manner, he too should live in complete harmony with society, and without hatred or malice. Seeing the events of the Universe ever proceeding towards a meaningful result, he realizes that man's life, too, must have a meaningful goal. Thus he exclaims: "O our Lord! You have not created (all) this without purpose." In brief, the universe being a manifestation of the Attributes of Almighty God is a real source of spiritual nourishment for those who want to lead a divine life on earth. They who attain that degree of spirituality which the *Quran* calls the "*Rabbani* soul" will be told, in the life Hereafter, by their most compassionate Lord: "Dwell in Paradise; You shall have no fear, nor shall you grieve" (7:49).

Spirituality in Islam has nothing mysterious about it. It is rather the direct result of the kind of intellectual development that takes place in the believer when he ponders over the Creator and His creation: what he gains in the process may be termed spirituality. The source of Islamic spirituality, therefore, is perusal and reflection rather than any mysterious exercise.

That is why the *Quran* rejects asceticism or monasticism,

refering to them as a *bidaa* (innovation) in religion which God did not prescribe for people.

The awakening of latent divine qualities in a person as a result of his observation and contemplation of the universe does not result in his shunning of normal life. Far from withdrawing from the world, he lives in it and participates in all its activities; yet despite his involvement, he remains aloof. He appears to live in the world, but stands apart. Thanks to this state of his heart, he acquires tremendous spiritual gains. The Prophet of Islam says of such individuals: "God plants wisdom in the heart of one who shows disinclination for the world."

The life of man is affirmed in his spirituality: this is the real life.

Swami Agnivesh

Enabling a just world

We stand on the threshold of a new millennium. This in itself is not all that important. What makes it a historic event is the fact that we are placed against a backdrop of a great human predicament that engulfs the world. None of us has had anything to do directly with engineering the emerging world order. It has presented itself as a *fait accompli*. But all of us, the six billion human beings that comprize the global community, are profoundly, even disturbingly, affected by it. The global developments in the last decade have precipitated enormous existential and spiritual questions that need to be addressed squarely. These issues have sharper edges for people in the non-western societies.

Words like globalization, privatization, liberalization, structural adjustment, market economy, and so on have wormed their way into the landscape of our mind. We catch the smell of the global order in our neighborhood. Its colors and sounds pour into our living rooms via satellites. The very feel of our environment has changed and our sense of independence is growing dimmer by the day. A feeling of being remote launched into unfamiliar, inhospitable economic and cultural orbits fills our intuitions with anxiety. It is as though pirates have boarded the ship of our collective destiny, and we find the loss of control deeply unnerving.

We in the East are not smart change-managers. It has been our problem for long. We have, besides, an uncanny knack for turning the means for empowerment into instruments of disability. That is what we have done, for example, with our religions. God was too generous to us in this one respect. Religions have been our main items of produce and export. They have done well in exile and explored new realms elsewhere. Buddhism is a good example.

However, at home we have degraded religion into a justification for oppression and exploitation, as in the case of the caste system, for instance. Bereft of our historical dynamism, we became inward-looking. As a religious person, a swami, I have no hesitation in recognizing that religions have failed human beings in their struggle for meaning and dignity, for justice and equity. That is not all. They have inflicted deep wounds on our psyche through their adversarial attitude, each to another. They have discredited themselves, besides, by their blindness to social realities. The common man no longer turns to religion for inspiration to become a better human being nor expects any public good to come from it. Escapist religiosity, however, now thrives more robustly than ever before! Temples, gurudwaras, mosques and churches, as well as sects and cults have multiplied and grown rich.

A century ago, Swami Vivekananda spoke euphorically about the spiritual destiny of India waiting to be fulfilled in the global arena and one which would benefit the entire human species. That dream and our deeds went their separate ways. Today, we have a global nightmare: a colossal split in the human condition – mounting poverty in the midst of multiplying wealth, escalating inequality in a world that resounds with the egalitarian rhetoric, unimaginable social injustice and man's cruelty to man, aggravated rather than ameliorated, by the freedom of a few and the enslavement of the rest.

The voice of Vivekananda reverberated in the citadel of materialism in an eloquent call to rediscover the lost spiritual vision of the human species. He saw it, primarily, as the fulfillment of the spiritual genius of India and then as the evolution of the human species as a whole. Much has changed since then. The precarious balance between materialism and the spiritual culture has only tilted further. The instruments of international control have gained unimaginable powers of coercion. The capacity of the poorer nations to resist the cultural onslaught on them has declined further.

At the same time, anxiety is mounting all over the world that, like the biblical Tower of Babel, the gigantic structures we have created could come crashing down and crush our future. In less than two decades, our honeymoon with globalization has begun to sour, paving the way for the realization that unless the global order is fortified by an appropriate and adequate spiritual vision it could turn into a gas chamber for our humanity. "Man," as Jesus Christ forewarned two millennia ago, "does not live by bread alone." It is a truth that continues to stare us in our face. Materialistic misconception to the contrary, offering bread at the cost of humanity, can only end up in multiple crises.

The first hymn of the *Ishopanishad* enjoins upon all human beings to enjoy material happiness in the spirit of sacrifice: *tena tyaktena bhunjithah* and then poses the fundamental question, *Kasya Swidhanam* – to whom does all wealth belong? It goes against the concept of private ownership of property. It is a very powerful exhortation to resist consumerism and capitalism, for our security lies in the shared well-being of all things that move or move not.

The vedic concept of *vasudhaiva kutumbakam* envisions the whole world as one family. It refuses to accept the world as a mere marketplace where everything gets commodified. Moreover, by molding human society on the family model of interdependence, it provides the guiding dictum: from each according to one's capacity, to each according to one's needs (and not greed). This of course is a different world-view from what we have today where individualism and a denial of the sacred dimension molds our thinking and action.

To create a world order, and not enunciate an appropriate spiritual vision for the global community, is positively suicidal. To throw nations and peoples of the world together in an economic pell-mell, without addressing the divisiveness and bankruptcy of religions, as they have been re-crafted in this century, is an act of irresponsibility. Why is that so?

To ask this question is also to ask what we mean by religion. Reduced to its essentials, religion addresses the question, as Tolstoy pointed out, of our vertical and horizontal relationships. In spiritual terms, this is to know and love God and to love one another. The joys and sorrows of our life are born of our relatedness. But the closer we get to people and groups the greater becomes the problem of their otherness. Proximity is a unique human paradox, given the fact that we are meant to be social beings. We need to belong. To belong is to come closer. But to come closer is to intensify the problems of differences. At a distance, differences do not offend. They hurt in nearness.

The recent communal turbulence in India illustrates this. More than in any other part of the world, different religious communities lived together in peace and harmony for long in the Indian subcontinent. But, of late, tensions between communities have intensified. Similarly, conflicts in every continent of the world have also multiplied and escalated in their violence. This is largely due to the greater proximity between religious communities effected by the age of communication and increased mobility. Knowledge is a category of nearness. You are not far away from what you know. Now the custodians of various religions know a great deal more about each other than they ever did before. Ironically, they know much less about themselves!

Yet, this increasing knowledge about each other need not necessarily aggravate the hostility of religious communities. What makes this otherwise desirable development a source of trouble is the fact that religions are still situated in a conflictual model following the prevalent world-view with its obsession with the "other." This gives an unfortunate slant to their interface. They look at each other in terms of differences and are blind to what they share in common. This creates a peculiar situation. The call of the times is centripetal; it pulls religions together. But religions in their attitude to each other are centrifugal; they pull away from each other. Till recently, when religions were confined to their separate constituencies, instability had been held at lower levels. It is at once ironic and significant that their growing nearness has raised tensions to levels of unprecedented violence.

In such a situation, religions can no longer afford to play their customary adversarial roles or try to thrive at one another's expense. Nor can they hope to prolong the uneasy truce by limiting their spheres of operation in the interest of communal harmony through a purely negative strategy. The land that was the former Yugoslavia or the vast tracts of the erstwhile Soviet Union bear testimony to this. Harmony, if understood only as an absence of tension because of the creation of ghettos, is hardly a spiritual value. Harmony of the dynamic kind calls for an active interaction among the religious groups and a shared forum for addressing the pressing issues of the global community. Vedic spirituality acknowledges and validates plurality of paths and traditions: *ekam sat, vipra bahudha vadanti*, Truth is one, but learned people call it by different names.

As we stand at the crossroads today, we can either be party to the tragedy of all non-western cultures and religions being stamped out by the dominant culture or turn to a new paradigm of plurality of perceptions. Religions could be relocated in a climate of mutual stimulation and shared commitment to human well-being. They could deepen their respective *spiritual roots*. The worth of religions would then no longer be measured in terms of the size of their respective communities but by the contribution they make to validate the sense of a shared destiny which the human species already feels strongly, for various reasons. However, for the poor and powerless societies of the world, the prospect of being incorporated into a homogenized world order ruled by a single system of values and morals is reprehensible. Justice and equity keep poorly in systems shaped by gross power. Spirituality can bridle power through a sense of fellowship.

What is spirituality? I understand spirituality to mean the attributes and operation of the Supreme Spirit, God. They are truth, love, compassion, justice, etc. These are the eternal values that underlie all faith traditions, and are at work as much in secular humanism as in Buddhism, Jainism and Marxism. Faithfulness to any particular image of God is not as important to me as the acceptance of these universal values which reflect the attributes of God. They empower us to resist untruth, violence and injustice. Spirituality needs to be recognized and valued, more so in its operations and practice in terms of its potential to transform action in the given context. It does not lend itself to academic exposition, for it is profoundly experiential and dynamic. Practical spirituality underlies the living concerns like universal human rights, responsibilities, duties and such norms. Spirituality is that which mediates the interdependence of creation and safeguards its sanctity.

The *Vedas* and *Upanishads* – scriptures, by and large only talk about *manurbhava* (being human) and not Hindubhava or Muslimbhava or Indianbhava or Americanbhava. Similarly, their teachings are *satyam vada, dharmam chara*, that is, speak the truth and follow *dharma* (the eternal: *sanathan* values). Swami Dayananda insisted, and Yogi Sri Aurobindo agreed, that the *Vedas* hold no historical or geographical bias but are universal in intent and significance.

Kanada, the proponent of Vaisheshika philosophy, defines *dharma* as *yato abhyudaya nishreyasa siddhi sa dharma*, whatever is good for this life and after-life is *dharma*. The details are left to be decided in a dynamic way by successive generations of people according to their situation in time and place. By its very nature, spirituality cannot be dogmatic about contextual details, the trappings of time and space. It may be noted in passing that, more often than not, conflicts and violence are engineered by making the trivial absolute, and by trivializing the Absolute.

Religion contextualizes and socializes the perennial and universal values. Being the manifestation of these values, religion needs to adapt its expression to different times, places and challenges. While the core remains eternal, the flesh and bones, the rituals and belief-systems must be flexible, adaptable, and not dogmatic. The role of a prophet, a messenger or a book is more honored if received and re-interpreted in a broad spirit and within the flow of life. The problem arises when a religion becomes a rigid and dogmatic belief system which is socially for the *status quo* and politically static. Then rituals and external trappings overtake the essential spiritual core. Religion then stands in danger of becoming a contradiction of the spiritual ferment that led to its own emergence. It becomes subservient to power interests and loses autonomy.

The problem also arises when, in order to achieve some quick results, well-meaning spiritual torchbearers play up miracles or promote superstition. While spirituality is different from material sciences, and acknowledges mysticism and experiences beyond the ordinary, the gullible masses are often deliberately led to believe in things highly irrational and dangerously illogical, such as witch-hunting, human sacrifice, sati, untouchability, incarnation of God: the last one replacing the true Universal God.

The only authentic universal vision that humankind has ever had of oneness and wholeness has sprung from the light of spiritual vision. It is doubtful if any of the great humanitarian international organizations would have come into being, but for the pattern that had already been pre-figured in spirituality. Unlike the mechanisms of institutionalized religions, the call of true spirituality has all along been to transcend the familiar boundaries drawn by the individual and the corporate ego, and to discover the wholeness that underlies the diversity of our world.

Thus, while one religion may look upon the other as its adversary, from a spiritual perspective, the other, even the enemy, is a part of the larger organic human species and therefore cannot be eliminated or excluded. This is the secret of the health and wholeness of a society. It is out of this sense of inalienable belonging to the whole that the principles of justice and compassion are born. Injustice, on the other hand, thrives upon a distorted view of otherness as a threat or a polluting entity. Thus, all through history, the tribes, castes, groups and races which have been subjected to systemic oppression have always been caricatured as sub-human groups or as sources of pollution. The charge of pollution, of desecration, is a religiously sanctioned rejection of the humanity of the victim. In such a context, true spirituality needs to assume a radical role. As Jesus of Nazareth said, "no Prophet is acceptable among his own people," and he himself unflinchingly addressed the problems of his own time and society.

The spirituality for the emerging global order cannot afford to be a compendium of nice and toothless sentiments. The oppressed and miserable people of the world have no use for such pious ornaments. They are not looking for improved cages. They are crying out for freedom. The heart of our global spirituality must, therefore, be an uncompromising commitment to social justice. Far from being an anthology of multi-faith dogmas or scriptures, spiritual maturity is, instead, the very base out of which the priorities and compulsions emerge and then evolve through an active engagement with the given context. It upholds the position of love for humankind and reverence towards God.

Spirituality is, therefore, the first source and resource for human empowerment. The free understanding of "empowerment" in the spiritual sense is not merely the ability to negotiate power-sharing, but also to transcend the power-paradigm itself. Every human being needs to be empowered to attain the fullness of his or her hidden human scope. Conditions for the full unfolding of the human potential in each person must be created. History bears witness to the fact that such a goal cannot be achieved within the current paradigm of power. The business of true spirituality, in the end, is for love to supersede power as the shaping paradigm for the human species.

The essence of the spiritual light that great seers have brought is the need for the human species to shift from the love of power to the power of love. Compassion, fellow-feeling, selfless commitment, a spirit of sacrifice and service, social justice, respect for human worth and human equality are all authentic expressions of the power of love; whereas the love of power sees them either as superfluous or as liabilities.

Vidya Rao

HATHAYOGINI

A work of art is a mirror. Whether this work of art is a performance of music or dance, or the creation of a painting or a sculpture, the artist holds up this mirror so that we may see ourselves in it.

Just such a work of art is a painting called *Hathayogini* by Gogi Saroj Pal. Looking at this painting, I have the most incredible feeling of recognition. I feel I know this woman, the yogini of the painting. Or is it a sense of reflection – is it myself that I see?

Perhaps this sense of recognition comes because *Hathayogini* poses – and answers – a basic question. How are we to be in the world? What is the nature and manner of our being?

I look at Gogi's painting, at the yogini. Here she is, seated on a tiger – or is it a tiger skin? – quietly powerful. This woman brings together the memories of older yogini cults, and Gogi's statement that even today, women can be, and are single-minded, purposeful, undivided, one unto themselves. And also that the yogini's single-mindedness, her purposefulness is different from the blinkered, goal-oriented race in which we have entrapped ourselves today.

Slight as she is, the yogini fills the frame of the painting. She occupies its space. Yet she does not aggrandize it. The space is

GOGI SAROJ PAL
HATHYOGINI

hers, because she is the space. She is not separate from it. And she looks straight out at you with clear, calm eyes. No sidelong glance, no coy, downcast eyes.

She sits straight and unmoving, and yet there is nothing rigid about her stance. Her legs are tightly locked in a yogic posture – energy is concentrated and held. And yet there is a sense of movement, flow. She is so light and easy, she might be dancing.

The *Hathayogini* is bare-breasted, but her body is not exposed for our viewing. Its nakedness is its nature, its truth. Her bare body is center frame, frontal, yet there is no sense of the voyeurism of the "center-spread." Nor is there any coyness. Her body just is. It is not displayed, it is not presented for viewing. And so it defeats the male gaze. It cannot be appropriated or consumed.

At her waist, skin-tones merge with red – is this then another embodying? Is this yogini a mermaid, a creature half human and half animal – or is she a *kinnari*, a half human and half divine being? Here, again, that fluidity in the way one color, one texture merges into another.

I look at her feet and see the stitched ends of the red. I see the red to be also a garment. And I see that her garment is as much a part of her as her skin. Her adornment, her *sringar*, is a part of her. It is not external, it is not put on. She is at once both clothed in the richest, most beautiful cloth, and naked as the day she was born. Skin and cloth merge into each other, exchange substance with each other. Cloth here is body, body is cloth, like Kabir's finely woven *chadariya*.

Red and green dominate this painting – the bright and the dark, the active, fiery, passionate warmth of red cloth, and the cool, quiet, watery background of green.

I look at the *Hathayogini's* eyes, so calm, yet so alive; so peaceful, yet so full of laughter. I see that she is completely herself, centered in her self, comfortable and at home, she needs nothing and no one. And yet her eyes are also warm and alive. The peace in her eyes does not come from a lack of interest in all that is around her. For her eyes tell us that she is alert, aware and engaging with the world. Her detachment does not preclude a loving involvement.

Perhaps this is why the yogini seems so familiar when I see

her. She is, for me, the essence of what it is to be a singer. I know her when I sing – in that moment when I am most deeply myself, centerd, yet moving, playing. She is indeed a mirror to us. We see ourselves here as we really are when we are most true to ourselves. *Hathayogini* is the embodiment of the Rig Vedic verse – two birds on a tree: one eats the fruit, the other simply witnesses.

This seeming paradox of simultaneous detachment and involvement, of eating the fruit and dispassionately observing – this is the very nature of our being. This is the manner of our being present in the world. This is how we are to live.

Sudhamahi Regunathan

TIME IN A COTTON BUD

> Unroll the scrolls of song
> raise the oyo strain
> unfold the music sheets
> this mother of ours,
> this native village with moss
> let it not be covered

The *Oyo Hoi Ya* is an eloquent ballad sung by the Adi-Gallong tribe living in the central part of Arunachal Pradesh. Built around the motif of cotton picking, this ballad sings of a woman's life: her joys, her sorrows, the inevitability in her life and the hope. Cotton picking tells the entire story of a village from the perspective of the spindle, the loom, the creativity and color, the symbolism of designs and the ultimate presentability of a family. Thus it brings a wonderful feeling of camaraderie among the women who perform these activities and has even inspired a world-view from the window of femininity.

Cotton picking is still an important activity amongst the women of the tribal community of Adis in central Arunachal Pradesh. Dwarf cotton shrubs yielding coarse short-staple wool are sown, scatter the *jhum* fields, away from the main crop under cultivation.

Each pod is picked when it bursts open to expose the white ball of wool. Every girl and woman goes out to pick the cotton at a time that is convenient to her and her cotton plant. Yet, without effort to organize the time, it brings the women of the village together, in the rhythm of plant and season.

The ballad begins with praise of the Mother Village. The identity of village as mother brings forth a host of similarities apart from the obvious one of fertility: the mother who sacrifices for them, who gives them shelter, who nourishes them, in whose lap they grow, whose land grows food for them. "Come," call the cotton-picking *oyo* girls, "come let us cheer her who toils for us all night and day, of whom we take endlessly. Let's make her life more colorful. Let's show her we care."

> Hi-yum yum-si-le
> Ane gu-min-si
> Gu-min hi-re-go
> Ir-men la-ju-ka

> Oh! This evening and now,
> our dear mother village
> with all your children, in gaiety,
> we come to warm and cheer you.

The word used for Mother Village, Gumin Soyin, is also the name of the deity of prosperity and good luck in Adi mythology. While the mother is celebrated as the deity of good luck, this ballad from a patriarchal community makes no mention of the father. A strong feminine bias indeed.

The call to celebrate goes out not just to those who are picking the cotton, but to women and girls everywhere, even those who are not "native born."

> Ne-li kom ji-e
> Ir-bam la-ju-ka
> Ne-ngo mo-bam-go
> Bum-mem la-ju-ka

> Girls not native born
> also those of tender youth

merry wives and guests on visit
come partake in common joy and cheer.

Even as the girls sing "we all come from our mother's heart, spring from her bosom like sprouts," a wave of sadness brushes the lyrics. Just as sprouts grow to become big trees and shrubs, and just as their branches are cut off, leaving behind the mother, so we too will have to move on ... move on to unknown villages, unknown lands, unknown fates, leaving our mother behind. It is sad, they sing, to watch the village as it loses the youth and beauty it has nourished. And they sing of this poignant experience of mothers and daughters:

We go to lands unseen
To places never known
to strange lands unknown
to lands where none have gone.
The pods of sesame burst
and the seeds are scattered far.
Arrows fly out of view
in the different directions shot.
From the old stem
from the ancient stalk
as new leaves grow
we too spring again from old stock.

And there is consolation. As the older girls leave, the new ones take their place. The Mother is recharged with the vitality of the young. So it is that this part of the ballad is called the "Old which always remains young." Rising to a positive note again, the call to celebration is repeated once more, for the old has to give way to the new and change is inevitable. It is in fact the very charm of life. Weaving the thread of continuity between the past, the present and the future, the singers depict the lofty idea of that which changes and that which is constant. Heed that which is constant, which endures longer and take change in your stride, they advise young girls, urging them to work and to till their lands for the fullness of each harvest.

The second part of the ballad tells the story of cotton

cultivation, how in the beginning, there was no cloth and how cotton gave them something to cover themselves with when mother earth gave them her land for the cotton to grow. The stages of sowing and watching over the growing cotton plant, come to an end with the plucking of full-blown pods:

Swells full and large;
the pods of cotton
swell full and large
and burst open
Oh the girls of oyo
start picking
continue picking ...

Yarn is spun from the cotton and then women sit at their low looms weaving their clothes. An ode to the creativity of the girls sings to their dexterous fingers that weave in fantastic designs – the designs and clothes that you wear as you dance around in gaiety while others watch you in admiration. The verses here are full of fun and reach a crescendo in frolic and enjoyment. Youth, glamor, life, vivacity all touch new heights.

For the girls of oyo
they wear to display
the dress to exhibit
worn for all to see
with an elegant sway
swinging to and fro,
in the heart of gumin
in the heart of soyin
with graceful sway
the charming round is done
the lovely maids of oyo
go prettily about.

The story of cotton, its sowing, the spinning of the yarn, giving it a shape and adorning it with design are likened to a bride: her birth, her growing up, her flowering and finally dressing up in the finery woven by the women of the village. And then when the fun is over, it is time for her to go away. The story has been told and retold, and ends with the same scene. It is also in these last stanzas of the second section that the deity is invoked. The stanzas speak of the women moving towards Dinyi, in all their finery. At one level the words imply marital status but at another, they imply a woman's spirituality ... an acceptance of life as it is, a surrender to the Supreme. They also emphasize tradition and the correct manner of doing things, and as they heed the codes of their tradition, the women move ahead in their lives. The ballad then offers reassurance – they will be happy, for the fun and frolic will come again, each year, inspite of some changes.

Is there a deep sigh, one wonders, as one reads the ending lines of the ballad?

When the brides are sent off
as the brides bid farewell.
When the girls as brides are brought
as they leave their own homes
this costume swinging in grace
will be put on.
In Dinyi's festivals
as the maids of Dinyi
the costume of swaying grace
will be put on
the costumes
will be put on.

Think not but that I know these things, or think
I know them not: not therefore am I short
Of knowing what I ought: he who receives
Light from above, from the fountain of light,
No other doctrine needs, tho granted true.
But these are false, or little else but dreams,
Conjectures, fancies, built on nothing firm.
The first and wisest of them all professd
To know this only, that he nothing knew.

John Milton, *Paradise Regained*

William A. Conrad

GOD AND THE SCALE OF EVIL

W hat are the factors which go against belief at the end of this millennium? How can traditional beliefs in the omniscience, omnipotence and benevolence of God, of any religion, square with certain actions in this world? The clearest example is the holocaust perpetrated by Hitler's Nazis on the Jews and other peoples. Some twelve million people were selected by virtue of who they were, then tracked down in cold blood and killed, then either incinerated in ovens or buried in mass graves. This action was a crime against humanity by any reasonable definition of what constitutes a crime. If God saw this, and he must have, and since God did nothing on a large scale to prevent this then it seems reasonable to assume He does not exist. For if He could have prevented the holocaust and did not, then who needs such a God?

It is the scale of an event that is constantly thrown into our face by the omnipresent TV in every living room, which prevents any belief. Personal tragedies and similar events on a small scale can be explained away as due to the need for individual freedom or as past *karma* or the lessons to be learned from them. However, on the scale of the holocaust, the mind can only conclude that there is something wrong somewhere. The simplest response is that the God of religion is a myth. There was not only the holocaust during World War II, but some thirty million soldiers and civilians were killed. Senseless killing on this scale did not cease with the war. During the partition of India some two million people were ruthlessly murdered for no reason except that they were Hindus or Muslims in the wrong place. In the last half of this twentieth century, ethnic and religious cleansing came in the aftermath of the breakup of the former Soviet Union with the numbers of victims in hundreds of thousands, as most recently in the former Yugoslavia. Africans have not been far behind with the Hutus and Tutsis of Rwanda among others, to say nothing of Pol Pot's decimation of the Cambodians.

The single element all these killings have in common, aside from their ferocity, is the large numbers involved. These numbers are a consqeuence, on the one hand, of the tremendous increases in population everywhere and, on the other, of the technological advances in the power of weapons. Perhaps the idea that "more is different" now applies to killings so that we need a new way of thinking about murder on the scale of millions. Or, *a la* Marx, quantitative differences become qualitative.

One common response to these thoughts is a loss of nerve which causes a person to retreat from the battlefield of life. This was the initial response of Arjuna at the battle of Kurukshetra when he looked at the fratricidal disaster which was about to begin. Krishna exhorted the despondent Arjuna: "Yield not to unmanliness, O Arjuna, it does not become you. Cast off this mean faint heartedness and arise, O scorcher of foes." We must face the brute, as Swami Vivekananda among others has said. There is no salvation in running away from life's battlefield. Christ is not known for his militancy, but he too said at one point, "I bring you not peace but a sword," to rouse his disciples' flagging spirits. We too must stand tall as we contemplate the evils of our century so as to not repeat them on the same scale in the coming centuries. Evil there will always be. It is for us to attempt to blunt its thrust and contain its reach.

If there is one human trait that is exploited by every tyrant whether petty or world-scale, it is the lack of self-confidence in oneself as expressed by Arjuna at Kurukshetra. Both words, "self" and "confidence" have to be contemplated and understood deep in the heart, in order to make the meaning operative. Self-confidence is the watchword of the future as of the past. A personal experience comes to mind. Working as a biophysicist in 1965 at St. Michael Hospital in New Jersey, I had the privilege of often being present in the operating room during open-heart surgery. Once I saw a young resident surgeon promoted for the first time, called upon to do the crucial cuts on the fused leaflets of a child's heart. His hands trembled, sweat poured from his brow, and I am sure, as Arjuna said in similar circumstances, his mouth was parched, his skin was on fire and he felt fear. At this point, the chief surgeon stopped the operation and said, "You may kill this child, but you must be detached." Without fearless detachment, he would, in fact, have been more likely to kill the child. The operating theatre is indeed a modern battlefield where all the techniques of self-control are necessary. Sadly, however, not always is there a chief who can stop the action to calm a person. And yet without this fearless, calm and detached poise one cannot perform the assigned task adequately. This self-confidence with fearlessness is indeed purity in action. No one who has been successful in any endeavor has lacked this confidence. History is a story of people who rose to the occasion by mastering fear – not of people who had no fears.

To come back to the question of scale, we may still ask: what role can religion play when its authority has been so undermined by the sheer scale of evil in the modern world? Let us look at action as the scriptures prescribe rather than to the reasons we commonly cite for action. Could such a change of perspective help us, and does it make sense? "Actions speak louder than words," goes the proverb. "By their fruits shall ye know them," says St. Matthew. Swami Vivekananda codified this idea as: "That action is good which purifies the heart and that action which makes us more impure is bad." The relationship between inner motivation and the outward action is a very complex one. Ultimately, there is no duality.

I have a friend whose husband has Parkinson's disease. The progression of the disease compels her to do more and more for her husband. I watch her as she grows in detachment as she performs the tasks, her actions driven by her love without any thought of return. Caught in this mill of her marriage, all selfishness is being ground out of her by the exercise of detached action.

In general, the purification of the heart renders one more loving and considerate to others, and in turn the process is helped by the action expressing it. This cycle strengthens our character and helps us to stand on the rock of truth, and our view of what is right becomes steadfast. It frees us from the tangles of personal desire and makes us willing to risk our own life, if necessary, to save another's. We act, not for the greater glory of God, but because the action in itself does good to us as the doer. The confidence in one's self and then the judgment of one's discriminating intellect improves with every action which purifies the heart. Unselfishness becomes a key factor in making a choice and thus one swings into a "holiness circle," which is the opposite of a vicious circle. Whereas the latter drags you down, the "holiness circle" spins you upward towards a holy goal, purifying you all the while.

The attitude that all these considerations suggest is a radical change within while nothing that is obvious alters. When I was new to spiritual life, my teacher told the story of a young monk of the Ramakrishna order who saw an old woman painfully collecting alms, grain by tiny rice grain. Suddenly, someone accidentally bumped into her so that all her painfully collected grains were scattered in the mud. The adept monk was so shaken by this stray incident that he went into seclusion for a week. On coming out, he was a confirmed non-dualist, but continued his acts of service as before. Nothing had changed but there was a transformation.

Perhaps we can follow the monk's response to small-scale evil to help change the way we respond to the sweep of large-scale evil that we are considering. We may start with the working hypothesis that we and all other beings are the unchanging Self, and that the goal of life is to realize that as a fact of experience. We approach every experience as an occasion to ask, "Is this what I seek?" and the answer is "No, not this, not this" (*Neti, neti*). Despite such an apparently chilling spiritual practice, the process is compatible with a life of service as exemplified by some of the monks of the Ramakrishna order. Their active life of service emphasizes the positive aspect of non-dualism – the Self in me is the same as in you. Service to others, which seeks to see the Self in them goes hand in hand with developing the discriminating vision to see that the world, as it is, is changeable and ultimately unreal. Together, these practices are self-reinforcing and form a holiness circle which spins you up to the Upanishadic realization "Thou art That." That realized, one can follow the example of Swami Vivekananda or Buddha and others who have lived and worked in the world, striving for the good of all beings, without being perturbed by the world.

Now what about the God of spiritual practice, not of reason? Let us face the scale of evil honestly. Krishna says in the *Gita* (11:32), "I am come as Time the waster of the people, ready for that hour that ripens to their ruin." In the Bible, God says, "I kill and I make alive, I wound and I heal and none can escape out of my hand" (*Deuteronomy* 32:39). Yet God never said anything about scale. God is also considered as benevolent, bequeathing mercy and unmerited good upon humankind, even answering unspoken prayers. These two contrary aspects are held separate in the mind. Yet, in the image of Kali she is depicted as two halves, one benevolent granting boons, the other malevolent destroying life. How can the human mind cope with the heap of *human* corpses, with purposeful killing on larger and larger scales?

I believe that if we juxtapose our concepts of God with the magnitude of the purposeful human evil that has been perpetrated in the twentieth century, the concepts of God would have to change. I cannot answer the questions that this must raise but I choose to make a change in my own thinking. When it comes to meditation, I choose to retain the image of a benevolent God. I recognize the contradiction, but knowingly choose to live with it until I can find an honest resolution.

I can still feel empathy for all those involved in holocausts without losing a sense of moral revulsion that murder on such a scale could actually happen. I hope that if I am presented with the precursor of such events, the memory of the past will give me the courage to stand up and say no.

Roger Housden

ORDINARY SPIRIT

It was for a year that I set my sail into the wind and let life blow me around this great country of the United States without an itinerary. Behind me I had left a home in England, and a love that – we both knew it, painful as it was – was wanting to take some other form than that of a couple, though we knew not what. I had a commission to write a book called "Sacred America"; my only compass was a predilection for individual experience over dogma and creed, and I trusted that to lead me wherever it would.

The journey really began in India – if anything begins anywhere. I had been in that wonderful, terrible country for several months in 1995, researching a book on the survival of the sacred in India. As I sat by the Ganges in the holy city of Banaras on my last day, the thought suddenly struck me – one of those thoughts that come from behind, or beyond the periphery of vision: India, for all its living spiritual wisdom, is not the land that holds the seal of the sacred for the next millennium. That country is the United States. From that moment on, the desire to explore that intuition for myself would not let me rest until I came here.

Such a wealth I encountered here of the spiritual kind, as would confound the preconceptions of both worlds – certainly the old, and even those of the new itself. The richness I found was not in any institution or religion so much as in the knowing spirit of individuals in every conceivable kind of life circumstance. Not on some public platform, nor in a monastery or a cave, but in ordinary life is where I found those who are living by a different tune: in financial offices, in the backcountry of Wyoming, on a bus in the Catskills, even in Hollywood. Each in their own way had recognized that life had its own intelligence, greater by far than any conclusions or choices we might call our own; and that by following that, they were not diminishing, but enhancing the individuality so precious to this culture. The story of one such individual, along with something of my own story, will serve to convey my meaning.

I first met Kristen Ragusen in, of all places, the Sahara desert. Occasionally I take small groups there to walk in silence for a week, a kind of ambulatory retreat. Kristen, who lives in Boston, had come on one of these madcap journeys earlier in the year, and it wasn't long before I noticed something unusual about her. Whatever the conditions – walking into a big wind, an especially cold night, the same soup every day for a week – Kristen would always respond with a smile. Not one of those smiles which hides something different, but an obvious acceptance of whatever life threw at her. She was twenty-nine then – a lot younger than many of the other participants – but it was often to her that people would talk when they were finding the going tough.

I learned that she was a financial consultant with Merrill Lynch, and that her joy and acceptance of life had grown not in spite of but because of her daily work with her clients and their hopes and anxieties over money. Her story intrigued me, and I wanted to hear more, but a silent retreat in the desert was not the right setting; so we agreed to meet when I next came to Boston.

I left Walden Pond in time to meet her at a restaurant the same evening. Kristen was at the table already, a slight figure with a shock of black hair tumbling down to her shoulders. When we had settled in I suggested that some might consider her kind of work – with an eye on the bottom line all day – to be at odds with a life lived in the spirit.

"Oh, but I don't see life to be divided like that," she laughs. "To begin with, my work is a continual voyage of self-discovery. For all the information we have, there are still no maps or strategies that will guarantee what the market will do today. I find it truly liberating to see that there is no way I can control or know the answer. When I really got that, I saw that there never could be any closure. Yet, problem solving and the desire to make people happy is so hard to let go of! I worked and worked, studied and studied. When I finally saw that it was impossible – how like a great ocean the market is – it was a huge release. That was one of the greatest spiritual lessons I ever learned. I had the freedom then to wake up in joy and know I can only do the best I can. The strange thing is, my performance has increased the more I have let go."

She paused for a moment, then resumed her flow of thought. "There's nothing like money to reveal people's values and their sense of meaning. My engagement with clients brings up the deepest questions. Who am I? Who are these people? Often they come in scared, excited, happy, guilty, all at once. Then, financial planning is itself a process of self-discovery – where are your priorities? what do you want to do in retirement? People are generally uncomfortable with knowing who they are other than as consumers of the American capitalist myth. I know that consumerism is filling a black hole inside, so I listen for the signs of that in their story. In them, I see the richness of who we all are, how our core issues are all the same."

I wondered how that might affect her, to see herself in the stories she listens to. "What it does is to awaken compassion in me – for them, for myself, for all of us," Kristen answered. "It's as if I sit there with them aware of two levels at once – the need to get the job done, and the beauty of who they are. I hear their financial concerns, but in essence I hear their wish to love and be loved. It's both a serious business and all so silly, and the two sides, each, need to be honored." She laughs again, a young woman's giggle. "Every day my work shows me how tied to the earth we are, and how free we are at the same time."

My desert intuition was right, I thought. This woman is

unusually free of the reactive mind. She must have learned this somewhere; steeped herself in some spiritual teaching that helps her be impeccable in the process of life, yet free of it at the same time. But no. Kristen is another natural, like Maria in Detroit. Kristen remembers crying out at the age of nine that she didn't want to be here. A white light appeared, moved towards her, and then faded away. She would have precognitive intuitions. Among her earliest memories is the experience of feeling our intrinsic oneness, and her work has returned her to this through a long and painful process of wearing away her resistances to playing the game.

She has been a financial consultant for several years now – but earlier on she would be so physically exhausted that her body would cry out; her mind would shrink from all she had to do in a day. It was a tough arena to play in, and at the end of the day a voice would wail, Why? Why? Then when she was twenty-two, she had a dream which changed her life. At the time she was feeling profoundly displaced, forsaken; even though, on the outside, she was already highly successful. She prayed for guidance that night, and cried for the first time in years. "If this is what life is about, it's not for me," she wept.

Kristen had – and still has – no particular Christian affiliation, but that night she dreamt she was in a classroom, and Jesus walked in. He walked straight up to her, his eyes full of love. His energy filled every ounce of her being. The attention made her feel guilty and shy, and she moved away, but he moved with her. Three times she moved away, she felt so unworthy; but each time, he followed her. The third time, she could finally accept his love. She was filled with bliss, and knew beyond all doubt that everything would be alright just as it was. He looked deep into her, eye to eye, and spoke about her later life. She felt so equal, so profoundly worthy, and she knew that to be his message for each one of us.

"When I recall the dream now," she added, "I still have the physical sensation that every tiny cell is loved and accepted; and that everything is exactly as it needs to be, no matter what. I have the sensation of a totally free and unconditional loving that is my ultimate security." With the popularization of depth psychology, dreams have once again come to be seen as a sacred language of the soul – a direct communication from worlds that are parallel to, though not separate from, the concrete one we live in. In a time of increasing spiritual autonomy, the authority of dreams has a significant role to play in the individual journey. I remembered my own being awakened one night, just before leaving England and the woman I loved, by a single image that filled me with joy for days. It was the smiling face of a radiant woman, ensconced in a scallop shell. It filled me with warmth, and I knew that although my loved one and I were parting, perhaps for ever, the feminine presence was alive inside me, and would nourish me through any dark days to come if only I would remember.

"From the time of that dream," Kristen was saying, "the tension around my work relaxed. The pain and fear of building my own business has again made me put my life into God's hands. The pressures are the same, but I sit with them now in a different way."

How would that show up in her daily relationships with clients, and with the market itself, I wondered? It's one thing to say that everything is in God's hands, and another to translate that into a concrete daily experience that is something more than fatalism.

"For one thing," Kristen responded, "I no longer want my clients to change. I used to want them to get my perspective more quickly, not to have their eye only on the numbers but rather on the bigger questions the numbers pointed to. I have let go of that now, which means I can really be with them as they are. When a new client comes in, I simply hold the question, Who is this soul? What do they cherish? That's where I go now, and the plan is simple then. At the same time, I do all I can to act impeccably within my role. We can never violate the play we are in. The two levels go hand in hand; they are different, but not antagonistic to each other. Again, my client list has risen dramatically since my own understanding changed."

When I asked her about her personal life, how it had been touched by the knowledge of love, she responded that she is aware in every part of her life of the intrinsically abundant nature of existence. Whenever she buys something new, she always gives something away. She always donates to her client's charities, and encourages them to invest in their own businesses, to have faith in their own enterprise. The point is, Kristen has discovered, the more she gives out, the more comes back in some other way. How do you see our financial situation collectively? I asked. Even George Soros, one of the biggest speculators out there, is saying the game can't go on.

"What I am seeing in our financial culture is a collective opportunity for spiritual awakening," Kristen answered. "And that will not be painless. The whole picture points to a showdown some time around 2012, when the baby boomers will be in retirement. People are living longer, while medical costs are increasing exponentially and more and more people will be drawing social security. College costs are increasing exponentially, currently around seven per cent annually, while inflation is running at three per cent. So we have these accumulating costs combined with the consumer's desire to feed the bottomless black hole, compounded with deflation and dropping returns on savings. The average fifty year old has just 2,500 dollars in savings. It will be impossible to sustain the consumer's hunger with a pittance like this, and that will inevitably fuel both a deeper questioning and a deeper despair. We shall have to start looking at self and community in a new way, because we just will not be able to satisfy our habitual feeding of desires. We will need to see collectively that we are not in control, and I believe the pain and sense of betrayal in that will bring about renewal."

I thought of the maverick philosopher, Terence McKenna, and how he has predicted that there will be a radical change in global consciousness around the year 2012. Kristen had not heard of him. She has simply drawn on her intuition and her knowledge of the statistics. The time had flown, and the restaurant had almost emptied. Before we parted I asked if her dream of Jesus was the only one to have marked her journey in such a significant way. She smiled and looked at me warmly. There was one other dream, she said; and she had had it in the Sahara desert.

"The main reason I came on your Sahara journey was to ask for guidance, for a reaffirmation that I was still on the right track," she explained. "It was several years since I had had that first dream, and I was beginning to wonder whether, after all, I would be better put to use in a working environment that more directly reflected my inner life. On the second night in the desert I dreamt that I was sitting at a table, when Jesus came in and pushed two oddly shaped stones towards me. I grimaced, hardly content with the message. He grimaced back at me, and said, Work with your stones. Be more specific, I thought; and he pushed the stones closer still. I looked at them, and knew the message was that I had been given the materials to work with; I had all I needed. I already have the raw working material to create what I'm here for, both inwardly and outwardly."

The next day, she wondered if she had misinterpreted the dream. As she walked into camp in the early evening, there in front of her were the exact stones of her dream. She almost didn't pick them up, seeing them simply as a blessing, a reconfirmation of her interpretation. Then she changed her mind, picked them up after all, and saw that they fitted perfectly into each other. She hadn't realized that in the dream – now she could see beyond all doubt that her material and spiritual life were one and the same thing.

"That is how I want to live my life," Kristen said as we parted. "I want to live in this world and use the tools I have been given: the realization that we are all one being; the release of expectation, the acceptance of people just as they are, an appreciation that our natural state is the abundance that flows from the creative and divine power that we are. Then I can see God, not in any outer spiritual practice, but in those stones, in the man who bags my groceries, in the person who just calls. In this lives the Great Peace; in this daily place of miracles."

I know that Peace, I thought, as I made my way to a hotel in Boston that night. Yet how easily it can be broken, I was reminded as I travelled the country over the ensuing months; how easily, rather, I fall from its grace into a state of forgetting. Then life is a struggle, and the way is hard. Several months after my meeting with Kristen, my research completed at last, I flew to Michigan for a month to start writing my book at the Fetzer Institute's Retreat Center. Just before I left San Francisco, they had phoned to say that they were overbooked for the first ten days, and that they had arranged for me to stay at a Christian Mennonite Retreat Center that was adjacent to their land. After those ten days, I could simply walk over the fields and stay with them.

So it was that I found myself opening the door of a converted barn in a remote corner of Michigan one summer evening. Two elderly Mennonites ran the center, and they had given me the apartment on the top floor. It was late, and they had left a note; I saw no one. In my journal that night I wrote about how relieved I was to be in one place at last; alone with a book to write, and the rest of my life before me. I could spend a year in a Buddhist or Christian monastery, I wrote; I could go to Bali for six months, or start a project in Africa. Anything was possible. I went down to lunch the next day – all meals were in silence – to find a long refectory table with the two Mennonites at one end and someone at the other end, with my place laid opposite. I sat down, looked up, and was met by – what else can I say? – the smiling eyes of unselfconscious love from a tall, erect woman with blond hair falling around fine chiselled bones and wide open eyes. The woman's gaze remained on me, showering me with a direct, uncomplicated warmth, as if she were welcoming a dear friend. My own soul felt present suddenly in the looking. I tried not to laugh; the Mennonites were eating their dessert, oblivious. I was filled with disbelief, incomprehension, and inexpressible joy.

Maria had arrived the day before me, and was there for ten days. We were the only guests. Two days after our meeting, I was looking at her out of the corner of my eye thinking, Who ARE you? Instantly she turned and said, laughing, "Haven't you recognized me yet?" After three days the old couple said they had to go away for a week. Would it be alright if we were on our own for that time? They would have someone come and cook meals for us.

Yes, it was alright that we were on our own for that time; though it took me a day or two to let Maria past my preoccupation with writing and to acknowledge that – even though the last thing I had in mind was an encounter such as this, the embers of my previous relationship still being warm – life had delivered me into a situation that I simply could not ignore. When I wasn't writing – I did try keeping to some sort of schedule – we spent the week walking the fields and the woods, hearing something of each other's stories – though with ample intervals of silence, Maria content to listen to the presence of the season among the trees. It began to dawn on me that I was in the company of a rare individual; one deeply trusting of the moment, who genuinely seemed to respond to everything and everyone – the cat, the housekeeper, the ants crossing her path, as well as to me – with the same unfettered warmth and embrace. She is the sun, I thought one day, glancing at her as we strolled up and over the meadow. She is the sun and she comes on strong. Sometimes I needed to shade my eyes. She liked candy bars too, and came from a suburban world in New Jersey, the like of which my own prejudices had kept me well away from all of my life. Yet a spring had broken out in Maria's heart somehow; or perhaps it had been flowing from the time she was born. She had her own native wisdom, undeniable at every turn.

When the time came for her to leave, we both acknowledged that our meeting had taken place entirely outside of the framework of ordinary time and space, and that it may have nothing to do with our everyday lives. So we exchanged no details. Maria's life in the world was not, anyway, without its complications. If the blessing of our encounter was meant to continue in time, then surely the intelligence that had brought us together would arrange for it to continue, without our having to manipulate circumstance.

Just as she was leaving, Maria gave me a card. It was Botticelli's Venus. Later that afternoon, I suddenly remembered: My God, the scallop shell! The face in the scallop shell that had woken me in England – of course – it was a face with all the hallmarks of Venus. And Maria, of all people, was Venus personified. I knew my life was on the edge of a whole new direction – I knew it, though I still couldn't acknowledge it then. I knew in that moment beyond any doubt that my life was not my own; that its unfolding was not in the hands of my daylight mind. There is a greater life that lives its way through us. We can open the door onto that deeper well or languish for decades in a prison of preconceptions. Perhaps even that – the languishing we all do at one time or another – is part of the same wisdom – is there any blade of grass that can lie beyond its pale?

Maria and I did meet again, and have continued to do so when time has life, even if we never meet again. Interpretation, I have come to realize, kills the golden goose. It veils the ongoing revelation of life even as it serves to reassure us that we know who we are and what is happening. Life will weave its own exquisite, if not always painless, symmetry – and all the more gracefully as I embrace it.

I tell this story to point again to the pattern of intelligence within which we all live and breathe. To keep faith with this larger picture we need not to abrogate responsibility to some higher power, but to live from the wellspring of authentic, individual being. Such faith connects the particular with the universal through resonance. It is a far cry from belief: belief is a conceptualization of the truth as one would like or wish it to be. There is a place for belief, yet belief is not faith. Faith, as lived by Kristen Ragusen in Boston, and by so many others I met on my American journey, is an unreserved opening of the mind to truth; to the dynamic force of Reality, however it may turn out to be.

It is a readiness to hear and live by that intelligence that I have found emerging all over this country. It is there in Reverend Michael Beckwith's words, when he said in Agape Church in Los Angeles that our purpose is to be present for the embodiment of something greater than ourselves, rather than trying to hoist ourselves into greatness. Jim Wallis, in DC, avoids burnout on his punishing schedule as a social activist by knowing that there is a grander design at work than his own; that, while doing all he can for what he believes in, he is not in control of how life turns out.

From salaam, the peace passing understanding at the heart of us all, declared Professor Sayed Nasr at the conference in Georgetown on the role of Islam in the next century, ensues a trust in the emerging process of life, at the same time as action for the greater good. It is the source of action because compassion naturally arises from wisdom, and wisdom is the nature of that peace. That peace, I discovered, is in the heart of countless ordinary individuals that I have encountered all over this surprising country. This larger life doesn't need dreams, visions, or spectacular events to make itself known. It happens anyway, anywhere, all the time; some of us just need a knock over the head to wake up to its voice. Life happens anyway, and it is inherently wise, however painful or joyful it happens to be.

Not only our personal lives, but the life of a culture, of the planet, happens with an intelligence inscrutable to our logical, even moral, minds. We all have a story – we can't not have a story and be in a physical body – and the story will have its way; our smaller, individual ones, and the bigger one we all share in. We are like the sandpipers on the beach, moving this way and that as a single wave; we are immersed in the depths of a conscious, living world. Our peace of mind is commensurate with our faith in the inherent purpose and wisdom of life as it emerges. Yet that wisdom is not located anywhere outside of us; no one is doing something to us; we are embedded in it, and serve to shape it through our conscious and willing participation. In some paradoxical way, it seems to me – both from my own experience and those of the people I have encountered – the more we live in that faith, the more we are free to be who we can be; and the more life opens into a greater fullness, ever surprising. As we exercise that freedom – so different to the imagined freedom of the ego – we begin to embody the essence of democracy; and in so doing, we contribute to the fulfillment of our culture's promise. Sacred America, I would suggest, is that increasing communion of souls who are living their lives, not by some external dictate of creed or culture, but by the promptings of the knowing heart – the original meaning of conscience. This, rather than yet more experts and priests, is the fertile ground for a leaderless spiritual emergence; for a truly democratic postmodernism of belonging and wonder.

Finally, I am reminded that the first true democrat was none other than a man called Jesus. Jesus lived that faith and freedom; he upheld the equality of women, but also of the poor and the criminal in the sight of God; he taught not from the book but from the universal wisdom of the broken heart; and his life and death were exemplars of the mystery of the Spirit. The Western spiritual tradition may yet find its full flowering beyond the confines of church and creed, in the hearts and minds of people of conscious faith. Which is what you might expect in the most practical, the most secular, and also, I have come to realize, one of the most spiritually vibrant cultures on earth.

Death be not proud, though some have called thee
Mighty and dreadful, for, thou art not soe ...

One short sleepe past, wee wake eternally,
And death shall be no more, Death thou shalt die.

John Donne, *Sonnet on Death*

The clay warns the potter,
Do not knead me dear,
beware that a day will come
when I shall knead you here.

Kabir

Makarand Paranjape

Na Hanyate, IT IS NOT SLAIN

There are always a couple of famous rotting corpses in the spiritual backyards of our literary imagination. There is, for instance, the corpse of Father Zossima in *The Brothers Karamazov*. A priest, a monk, a holy man of the highest rank, a well-loved leader of the church, whose own life has been exemplary, Zossima's body is expected to preserve well. There may be no church promulgation to this effect, but that is the popular belief. By the afternoon of the next day, however, the odur of corruption is all too evident, slowly seeping out of the chamber of death like an incubus. Even the most faithful followers of the deceased elder cannot deny it. Why is God testing their faith, they wonder. Soon, tongues begin to wag. There is a minor rebellion brewing in the monastery. Zossima's teachings must be false, some of the doubters aver. Young Aloysha, the guileless, faithful, devoted Aloysha, who so doted on Zossima, is perplexed too. When Ratikin tauntingly asks him, "But, surely, you're not so upset because your old man is stinking the place out? You didn't seriously believe that he'd start pulling miracles out of the air?" all poor Aloysha can do is to reply: "I did believe, I do believe, I want to believe!" Ratikin mocks him farther, "So, you're angry with your God now, are you?" Aloysha says with a sudden, wry smile, "I haven't taken up arms against God, I simply don't accept his world."

Was the putrefying corpse of Zossima really a sign from the heavens? Did it symbolize the end of an older order of faith and belief? Was Dostoyevsky presaging a new era of atheism and anarchy, an age in which horrible crimes would be committed in the name of history, an epoch of concentration camps and torture chambers? As he himself wrote in a letter to Katkov, the editor of *The Moscow Herald*, "our socialists ... are conscious Jesuits and liars who do not admit that their ideal is the ideal of the coercion of the human conscience and the reduction of mankind to the level of cattle." Yet, in his own time, few supposed that Dostoyevsky was warning his country against the danger of the new, secular ideologies that were invading Russia from Europe; even fewer readers understood that he was advocating a return to the orthodox, national church of Russia as the answer. Years later, after the demise of the Soviet Union and the dismantling of the Berlin wall, Dostoyevsky's political perspicacity seems utterly breathtaking. True, the "devilishness" of Stalin may not have exactly resembled that of Stavrogin. While the latter's was a personal, inner, moral corruption, the former created a system which could truly be considered diabolical. Indeed, it was on seeing the smooth, white, embalmed hands of Stalin, as he lay in state in his coffin, that Marquez decided similarly to equip his dead dictator, the amalgam of all the despotic rulers of South America, in *Autumn of the Patriarch*.

Any way you look at it, the crisis of faith looms large over the modern world.

Sometime or the other, most of us have cried out in the anguished and desperate tone of Hawthorne's Goodman Brown, "My Faith is gone!" Brown, against the admonitions and pleas of his newly wedded wife, also called Faith, has ventured into the forest on a secret and shameful errand. He has followed a familiar figure, who in fact resembles his own father. On the way, he is astonished and frightened to see such personages as Goody Cloyse, who taught him his catechism, and Deacon Gookin, the very image of probity and piety, also hastening to the Devil's Sabbath. Not only are a great many of the good, decent, and respectable folks of New England society there, but even someone who resembles the Governor's wife. And yet, Brown believes that he can resist the Evil One: "With heaven above and Faith below, I will yet stand firm against the devil." But in the multitude of saints and sinners in the forest clearing, he thinks he hears the voice of his wife. "Faith!" he shouts, "in a voice of agony and desperation; and the echoes of the forest mocked him crying – 'Faith! Faith!' as if bewildered wretches were seeking her, all through the wilderness." Just when Brown thinks he has imagined it all, down comes fluttering through the night air, a pink ribbon, such as Faith had worn that very night. "My faith is gone!" Brown cries, "There is no good on earth; and sin is but a name. Come, devil! for to thee is this world given."

What happened to Brown in the forest? In his dark night of the soul, was the world revealed to him in its true, fallen state? Or did he simply have a bad dream, a nightmare? Whatever it was, it changed him forever. When he returns to his village at the end of the story, he is no longer the carefree and naive young yeoman who went into the forest on an unholy errand: "A stern, a sad, a darkly meditative, a distrustful, if not a desperate man, did he become, from the night of that fearful dream." Having seen evil within himself, he doesn't let it go, but clings on to it, projecting it outwards upon the whole world. Regarding everyone around him as evil, he dies a sad, lonely man, whose "dying hour was gloom."

The Puritan mindset is too simple, too reductive to contain contraries. It usually constructs the world in sets of binary oppositions: God/Satan, white/black, good/evil, virtue/sin, and so on. It denies the grey, the ambiguous, the doubtful. In its efforts to devise a world full of security and certitude, it simplifies reality to a formula. Armed with such a ready reckoner, it assaults life with enormous confidence and vigor. Its successes are great, but so are its failures. It lacks negative capability, the ability to negotiate contradictions. To it, faith is a matter of obedience, of submission, of utter lack of choice. Just as there is no escape from the original sin, grace too is irresistible – but only for the elect, the chosen. Faith is a deadly serious business, a matter not only of life and death, but of everlasting life and eternal damnation. No wonder that even today, the vast hordes of believers, the huge flocks of the faithful should so easily veer towards fanaticism and fundamentalism. The opposite of this faithfulness is the faithlessness, nihilism, extreme scepticism, and alienation of the modern condition. In this obverse world, God is dead and man is condemned to be free.

Between these two extremes, is there a choice, a third way, a different path?

Away from Europe and America, in the remote brahmin *agrahara* of Durvasapura in Anantha Murthy's *Samskara*, there is another rotting corpse. The anti-Brahmin Naranappa suddenly dies, leaving his brahmin community in a disarray. These brahmins didn't know what to do with Naranappa when he was alive; in his death, he poses an even bigger challenge to the *agrahara*: "Alive, Naranappa was an enemy; dead, a preventer of meals; as a corpse, a problem, a nuisance."

Naranappa has broken every rule in the book. He has been a meat-eater, a wine-swigger, a fornicator; he has kept a prostitute in his house, fished from the sacred temple tank, thrown the sacred ancestral *saligrama* into the river. He has vowed to destroy Brahminism. Now, in his death, his threat seems to have come true. Even the learned and saintly Praneshacharya doesn't know what to do with the body. Naranappa's death rites have to be performed, but who will do them? Naranappa has no children and though he has renounced brahminhood, brahminhood hesitates to renounce him. Praneshacharya cannot find the answer to this dilemma in any of the ancient books. He fasts and prays before Maruti, the village deity, but to no avail.

Instead, on his way back to the village, he stumbles into Chandri, Naranappa's concubine. Before he realizes what is happening, they couple in forest clearing. At midnight, the ascetic Praneshacharya wakes up: "A night of undying stars, spread out like a peacock's tail.... Green grass smells, wet earth ... and the smell of a woman's body sweat. Darkness, sky, the tranquillity of standing trees." The *acharya*, nearly forty, married out of choice to an invalid for almost twenty-four years, knows a woman for the first time in his life. Is it all a dream? But when he wakes up the next morning,

Praneshacharya feels like a man lost to himself: "For the first time, a desolation, a feeling of being orphaned, entered his inmost sense." Without knowing it, he has now become a kin to Naranappa, his dead, demonic adversary. He remembers a Sanskrit chant, "I am sin, my work is sin, my soul is sin, my birth is in sin." What should he do? How should he face the brahmins of the *agrahara* waiting for his verdict?

The starving brahmins, waiting for their leader, present a sorry spectacle. Vultures and crows, birds of ill omen, seem to have invaded their village. The hapless men strike the gongs and blow their conches to ward off the scavenging birds. The din and clamor can be heard in neighboring villages, who, ironically, only think that the pious brahmins of Durvasapura are at their daily worship and rituals again. But, unbeknownst to them, a terrible fate awaits the *agrahara*. Naranappa has brought the plague to their idyllic little village. There are dead rats everywhere. Dead rats and one reeking corpse, with which they don't know what to do.

Clearly, Naranappa's festering body is a symbol of the larger malaise that threatens to engulf the brahmin village. It has brought the plague of faithlessness to this brotherhood of the chosen. Even their leader, the saintly Praneshacharya, is nonplussed. He doesn't know what to do. Worse, he finds refuge and solace, quite accidentally, in the arms of Naranappa's mistress. Neither Praneshacharya nor the other brahmins of the village realize what has actually happened to them. The shadow of the black death of faithlessness has fallen upon them.

If anyone has her bearings, it is Chandri, the low-caste, "fallen" woman, who has been Naranappa's keep for ten years. While the brahmins are fasting on account of the pollution caused by Naranappa's death, she walks to the plantain grove and feeds herself. She nurses and comforts the poor, starving, and distraught Praneshacharya, when Maruti gives him no answer. On her return to the village, she heads straight for Naranappa's house. Instantly, she realizes that what lies there is, more than anything else, a dead body that must be attended to: "That was not her lover, Naranappa. It's neither a brahmin nor shudra. A carcass. A stinking, rotting carcass." Acting swiftly, she enlists the help of a Muslim friend of Naranappa's. Together, they cremate the body, without the knowledge of the confused, distraught brahmins.

I think we should follow Chandri's example. Good faith soon becomes bad faith. When that happens, it assails us like a decomposing corpse. We must then do what is demanded of us – cremate the corpse of the old, broken faith and dive into the vast ocean of truth. Simply speaking, there are no guarantees in this world: God may fail us, the Guru may fail us, and we may fail ourselves. Our job is to confront and face the truth, the reality of our existence, not to believe in half-truths and half-lies. Faith is not about dwelling in the Elysian fields of comforting illusions, but about swimming in a whirlpool of discomforting truths. It involves an engagement with life, with people, with reality. Faith is about being free and fearless, not about trying to hide behind doctrines to escape from suffering.

To understand the mystery of faith, we have to learn a fundamental lesson. Faith in something – anything – is bound to be transient, limited, prone to error, susceptible of decay and death. The object of faith, no matter how cleverly we define it, is always imperfect. An imperfect object cannot sustain a perfect faith. The deeper reason for this difficulty will be clearer when we shift our attention to the subject of faith. This subject is unreliable, fickle, transitory, and ultimately, insubstantial. It seeks to perpetuate its regime of separateness by identifying with something that is more reliable, less transient than itself. But no matter what it invents, that invention will bear the taint of its inventor, will have to share its partiality and dissatisfaction. As embodied beings, how can we overcome this problem of inadequacy, of incompleteness?

It is only when faith is reposed not in something or the other, but begins to manifest itself as the very medium of our existence, the essence of our being, the stuff of life, that it becomes meaningful. This kind of faith is not necessarily unwavering or unreasoning. Nor is it blind or absolute. It is not unquestioning belief, nor is it a system of beliefs or dogmas. It is closer to a confidence, a trust, a reliance, not in something, but as a sort of commitment to truth, if you will – to that which is, which is not an idea or a thought, but the very stuff of existence.

The Sanskrit word for faith, or close to it, is *shraddha*. The *Bhagvad Gita* has many passages extolling the virtues of *shraddha*. Without *shraddha*, Krishna says that true knowledge is not possible: "One who has deep faith gains divine knowledge, being full of zeal and devotion to it, and endowed with the mastery of the senses. Having attained that knowledge he is soon established in supreme peace." (4.39) Here faith is seen as the prerequisite for that knowledge which brings peace. Faith is therefore something that prompts right perception and action. But it is in one of the creation stories of the early Vedic lore that we find a really fascinating account of *shraddha*. In this myth, Shraddha and Manu are the progenitors of humankind. Manu, or the one endowed with mind, is the father, while Shraddha, or faith, is the mother. Shraddha, interestingly, is the daughter of Kama or the life-principle. Kama is not just desire or eros, but the creative force which seeks to express itself through life. It is that power, like the primal energy, which is responsible for all activity, all becoming. That is why, in Jaishankar Prasad's great epic, *Kamayani*, Shraddha is called Kamayani, the daughter of Kama. Shraddha or faith, is thus the determination of the life force to manifest itself. That combined with the conscious mind makes up the human being.

This is a myth which contains a deep truth. The truth is that faith is natural to the human condition. We humans are creatures of faith. It is a part of the design of creation itself. There may be an individual defeat or death, but not a collective end to human aspirations. Nature is careless in her plenitude. She allows all kinds of experiments, all sorts of permutations and combinations. Through every possible setback or obstacle, she persists. Ever and anon.

Faith, then, is native to us. Life itself would perish without it. It informs every action of ours; it moves us in everything we do It is faith that leavens our spirit to rise, to grow, to evolve. Faith is not something alien to us, something we should desire or inculcate. It is that which motivates all our fumbling, groping, and reaching out. Faith, like life, is indestructible. This is not faith in something or someone, but faith as the very essence of our being, the very stuff of our existence, the very marrow of our bones.

Therefore, there is no such thing as worry about losing faith. Faith is anterior to any gain or loss; it is one with life. As long as life persists, so long will our faith last, in one form or another, in one way or another.

I shall end, as I began, with a literary anecdote. Madhu Tandan's *Faith and Fire* is a powerful, moving, real life account of a young couple's experience in a remote ashram in the Himalayan foothills. The couple, giving up the world, has undertaken a life of spiritual discipline under a famous Guru. The Guru, however, is responsible for a number of disciples, one of whom he is grooming as his successor. The heir-apparent, from his own insecurities, takes a dislike to this couple. The result is that they find themselves gradually shunned and isolated in the small community, which is their only refuge. The Guru, to all appearances, continues to shield and support his successor in a manner which seems totally unfair to the narrator-protagonist. Finally, there is a break. The couple, very painfully, decides to wrench itself from that community and return to the big city. There is a decisive encounter with the Guru in which he listens to their side of the story in silence. Finally, he says, "An overdose has been given ... an overdose of pressure ... something may have died." Then, gazing out of the window and being silent for ten minutes, he adds, "If mistakes have been made, I'll pay for them."

What do these words of the Guru mean, the narrator wonders. Do they mean that the Guru's protection is still over her head? Does it mean that, in some way, the Guru himself brought on this rupture? The book ends with the author's dream in which she experiences the Guru's great love and protection. The ambiguity about the meaning of the dream, however, persists. She will never know for sure, because a year or so after her return to the city, the Guru passes away.

The spiritual life is no bed of roses; rather, to use another metaphor, it is walking on the razor's edge. I respect those, whose faith is strong, who trust in God, Guru, or some ideology; who, moreover, live according to their betrothals and commitments. I also respect those who question every certitude, who are doubters and sceptics, who seek only the truth, not any illusion that masquerades as truth; who, moreover, have faith in themselves and take responsibility for their own lives to the best of their abilities. A faith which is never tested is no faith at all; a faith for which one doesn't put one's life on the line, is not worth holding on to; a faith that comes too easily will not stand the stress of life. Only a faith based on recognition, understanding and direct apprehension of reality will remain steadfast in adversity. Such a faith is fearless and free, not timorous and fettered.

Though I do not have such faith yet, I do not wish to substitute it with anything less. Perhaps, what I offer is nothing – no great solace or carnival of hope. And yet, what remains after the content of experience has been exhausted, is not a nihil, not an abyss, not a negation merely, but something that is quiet, gentle, a murmur of compassion and peace perhaps, an emptiness that has been cleansed of false pieties and platitudes, and therefore fit for the reawakening of faith.

Works Cited

Anantha Murthy, U. R. *Samskara*. Trans. A. K. Ramanujan. New Delhi: Oxford University Press, 1977.

Dostoyevsky, Fyodor. *The Brothers Karamazov*. Trans. David Magarshack. Harmondsworth: Penguin, 1958.

Hawthorne, Nathaniel, *The Scarlet Letter and Selected Tales*. Great Britain: Penguin Books, 1970.

Tandan, Madhu, *Faith and Fire*. New Delhi: HarperCollins India, 1997.

Like sheaves of corn he gathers you unto himself.

He threshes you to make you naked.

He sifts you to free you from your husks.

He grinds you to whiteness.

He kneads you until you are pliant;

And then he assigns you to his sacred fire, that you may become sacred bread for God's sacred feast.

All these things shall love do unto you that you may know the secrets of your heart, and in that knowledge become a fragment of Life's heart.

But if in your fear you would seek only love's peace and love's pleasure,

Then it is better for you that you cover your nakedness and pass out of love's threshing-floor,

Into the seasonless world where you shall laugh, but not all of your laughter, and weep, but not all of your tears.

Love gives naught but itself and takes naught but from itself.

Love possesses not nor would it be possessed;

For love is sufficient unto love.

Kahlil Gibran
The Prophet

MYSTICAL DRAWING BY KAHLIL GIBRAN

Notes on Contributors

AGNIVESH, SWAMI, could be called a monk with a mission. He has devoted his life's energy to struggle against social injustice which is too often perpetuated by religious dogmatism, bigotry, racism. He pioneered movements in Haryana, UP and Rajasthan and successfully challenged the practices of bonded labor and child labor and testified before the United Nation's working group on Contemporary Forms of Slavery at the UNHRC in Geneva (1988-9). The Swami is an active participant in interreligious dialogues and exchanges and strives to bring together all constructive efforts for establishing a liberal and egalitarian society under the banner of "Religions for Social Justice." He received the Anti-Slavery International Award, 1990, London, and the Freedom and Human Rights Award, 1994, Bern. He has authored *Vedic Socialism* (Hindi) and *Religion, Revolution and Marxism* (Hindi and English) and contributed papers and articles to various newspapers and journals.

ARMSTRONG, KAREN, is known worldwide for her international bestseller, *A History of God*. Her new book, *The Battle for God: Fundamentalism in Judaism, Christianity and Islam* was published in Spring 2000. In the 1960s she spent seven years as a Roman Catholic nun but left her teaching order in 1969. Since then her work as scholar, writer and television broadcaster has kept her actively involved in the living issues of religious experience and inter-religious encounters in the Western world. Her books include: *Through the Narrow Gate: A Memoir of Spiritual Discovery*, an autobiographical work, *The Gospel According to Woman: Christianity's Creation of the Sex War in the West; Holy War: The Crusades and their Impact on Today's World* and *Muhammad: A Biography of the Prophet*. Most recently she has published *Jerusalem: One City, Three Faiths* and *In the Beginning: A New Interpretation of Genesis*. Her books have been translated into thirty languages.

BRAYBROOKE, MARCUS, is the vicar of Marsh Baldon, Toot Baldon and Nuneham Courtenay, three villages near Oxford. He has been a central figure in the world's interfaith activity which he has pursued for more than thirty years. He joined the World Congress of Faiths in 1965, has been editor of *World Faiths Insights* and is presently its Joint-President. He has been particularly concerned about establishing links between interfaith organizations internationally. He is a trustee of the International Interfaith Centre, the International Peace Council and the Council for a Parliament of the World's Religions. He has authored and edited several books which include *Pilgrimage of Hope*, and the more recent one, *Faith and Interfaith in a Global Age*, both books highlighting not only the necessity of interreligious understanding but also the exciting opportunities for attaining such understanding at meaningful levels.

CAREY, JOHN, lives and teaches in Ireland at the University College, Cork, in the Department of Early and Medieval Irish. He received a doctorate in Celtic languages and literatures from Harvard University where he taught for some years before heading for Ireland. He has held fellowships at the Warburg Institute (University of London), the Institute of Irish Studies at the Queen's University of Belfast and the Dublin Institute for Advanced Studies. He has published extensively in journals devoted to Celtic studies, medieval studies, and comparative religion, and is the author of *King of Mysteries: Early Irish Religious Writings* and *A Single Ray of the Sun: Religious Speculation in Early Ireland*. He is a fellow of the Temenos Academy, and serves on its Council and Academic Board.

CHAKRABARTI, ARINDAM, has explored the question of faith both intellectually as well as in the living tradition of a *shishya*, disciple. He studied philosophy at Presidency College, Calcutta, and St. Anne's College, Oxford, completed his doctoral work in philosophical logic under Sir Peter Strawson and Professor Michael Dummett, and later trained in Navya Nyaya under Pandit Vishvabandhu Tarkatirtha. He is currently with the University of Hawaii at Manoa and is associate editor of *Philosophy East and West*. He was the first Indian to deliver the Manto Lecture on South Asian Theories of Violence at the India International Centre in 1999. Besides numerous philosophical papers, Chakrabarti has authored *Denying Existence*, and has co-edited *Knowing From Words*, with the late Professor Bimal K. Matilal.

CONRAD, WILLIAM. A., a biophysicist by training, has been associated with the Vedanta Society of New York since 1955, and is an editor of the magazine *American Vedantist*. During World War II he was in the US Air Force as a navigator on a B24. He flew some twenty-five missions before the last one in which the engine of his aircraft shot over the target, but he and his crewmates were able to get to Petropavlovsk on Kamchatka, off the Bering Sea and were interned there until the war in Europe was over. During the five years he spent in Europe, partially on a Fulbright Scholarship, he came in contact with the ideas of the East after reading Mahatma Gandhi's autobiography. He has also studied *hathayoga* and practices meditation.

EICHERT, DONALD, was born in England, the grandson of German immigrants, and read philosophy at Oxford. He worked as a journalist in Canada until 1962, when he settled in India and took initiation from Sri Krishna Prem. In 1977 he became an Indian citizen. He worked as a journalist and editor of science books until 1982, when he and his Indian wife moved to Mirtola ashram. They returned to city life shortly before her death in 1997. He is the author of *World-Pictures*, a philosophical novel.

GISPERT-SAUCH, FR. GEORGE, is a Spanish Jesuit theologian whose areas of interest center on the meaning of faith and include the context of the historical and theological contacts between Hindu and Christian traditions. He came to India in 1949 and studied philosophy and theology in the Christian institutions here, and Sanskrit and Pali at the University of Bombay. He received his doctorate in theology from the Catholic University of Paris for his work on the Vedic concept of *Ananda*. His subsequent teaching and writing career developed at St. Mary's College, Kurseong, which later shifted to Delhi as the Vidyajyoti College of Theology.

HALDANE, JOHN, lives in Scotland and belongs to its life, engaging in public issues with the sense of truth of a *gyani*, man of learning. He is Professor of Philosophy, and Director of the Centre for Philosophy and Public Affairs, at the University of St. Andrews, Scotland. He is also a Fellow of the Royal Society of Arts, a Fellow of the Royal Society of Edinburgh, and an executive council member of the Royal Institute of Philosophy. He is Stanton Lecturer in philosophy and religion at the University of Cambridge for 1999-2002, and in 2003-4 he will be Gifford Lecturer in natural theology at the University of Aberdeen. He has published over a hundred and twenty academic papers covering areas such as: the history of philosophy, philosophy of the mind, metaphysics and moral and social philosophy. He is co-author of *Atheism and Theism*. His latest collection of essays being published are *Faithful Reason* and *An Intelligent Person's Guide to Religion*.

HOSKOTE, RANJIT, is a poet, art critic and commentator on philosophy and cultural history. He has written and lectured extensively on the turbulent relationship between the sociology of religion, the politics of ethnicity and the pressures of globalization in a post-colonial environment. He has also attempted to explore the competing claims to civilizational identity that come to be asserted in such a historical context. During the years 1993-9 he had conceived and edited a popular column on philosophy and spirituality called "The Speaking Tree" for the *Times of India*. He now works for the *Hindu*. Hoskote was a Visiting Writer and Fellow of the International Writing Program of the University of Iowa, USA, 1995, and recipient of the Sanskriti Award for Literature, 1996. His publications include two volumes of poetry, *Zones of Assault* and *The Cartographer's Apprentice*, as well as *A Terrorist of the Spirit*, a translation of the Marathi poet Vasant Abaji Dahake's *Yogabhrashtha*, and *Pilgrim, Exile, Sorcerer: The Painterly Evolution of Jehangir Sabavala*, a critical biography of the distinguished artist.

HOUSDEN, ROGER, author of eight books and a leader of contemplative journeys in the Sahara and in India, takes seriously the words of the poet, Mary Oliver: "Are you breathing just a little and calling it a life?" Oxygen is his favorite food. A student of the spiritual traditions of India for over twenty years, he published *Travels Through Sacred India* in 1996, as a traveller's guide to the sacred life of India. He has recently published *Sacred America: The Emerging Spirit of the People*.

KHAN, MAULANA WAHIDUDDIN scholar and theologian, has won recognition for his advocacy of peace and interreligious harmony. He graduated from a seminary of traditional Islamic learning and then turned his attention to modern thought. In the course of his research in religious and modern scientific fields, he came to the conclusion that there was an urgent need to present Islamic teachings in the contemporary scientific idiom. His book, *Religion and Modern Challenges*, was translated into Arabic under the title of *Al-Islam Yatahadda*, and came to be accepted as a standard work on Islam vis-a-vis the modern sciences. He established the Islamic centre in Delhi in 1970. *Al-Risala*, the organ of the center, was launched to awaken in Muslims a new awareness of their social responsibilities. He has published over one hundred books, and a two-volume commentary on the *Holy Quran*.

NAIPAUL, V. S., Nobel laureate for Literature, 2001, has been sometimes called the writer's writer. He was born of Indian ancestry in Trinidad in 1932. He came to England in 1950, spent four years at University College, Oxford, began his writing career in 1954 and has never looked back. He has pursued no other profession and his novels, beginning with his very first, *The Mystic Masseur* (1957: John Llewellyn Rhys Memorial Prize), have won every major literary prize in English including the Booker in 1971 for *In a Free State*. An important part of his prolific work derives from experiences of travel among people of diverse cultures of the world, including the two acclaimed titles: *Among the Believers: An Islamic Journey*, 1981, and *Beyond Belief*, 1998. His most recent book is *Letters Between a Father and Son*, and his latest novel, *Half a Life*. V. S. Naipaul received a knighthood in 1990.

PAL, GOGI SAROJ, arrived on the contemporary art scene around the 1970s, bringing with her a family tradition of social reformers, freedom fighters and writers, and her own compulsion to give expression to her story through art. She works in varied mediums: installation, painting, sculpture, graphic print, ceramics, jewelry, weaving, photography and computer. She has participated in dozens of national and international exhibitions and has organized twenty-six solo exhibitions of her work. She was awarded the Sanskriti Award in 1980, the jury's commendation in the International Biennial of Plastic Arts at Algiers in 1987, the National Award in painting by Lalit Kala Akademi in 1990, and has also won an award in the Cleveland Drawing Biennial in 1996.

PANDEY, ALOK, a professional psychiatrist, is a serving officer with the Indian Air Force. He has also been for long a devout student of the writings of Sri Aurobindo, his guru. His work (as a medical professional) and his *sadhana* come together to seek a fresh perspective on human nature and its condition. He is co-editor of *NAMAH* (New Approaches to Medicine and Health), a quarterly journal published by the Sri Aurobindo Society, Pondicherry, and member of a team working on a new paradigm for viewing the future. His writings and talks cover themes of yoga, education, psychology and health.

PANIKKAR, RAIMON, is a person difficult to introduce. He could well be the world's leading scholar of comparative philosophy and religious studies. He lives in the mountains of Catalunya in Spain. A Catholic priest, thinker and seeker of wisdom, Panikkar himself partakes of pluralistic traditions: Indian and Spanish, Hindu and

Christian, sciences and humanities, and writes books and articles in six languages. He has taught at universities in India, Europe and America: Sanskrit in Madrid, philosophy in Rome, Indology in Bangalore and comparative religion in California and Harvard. He has lectured on Indian philosophy, culture and religion in Latin America. Currently Professor Emeritus at the University of California, Santa Barbara, he has published over forty books including *The Vedic Experience: Mantramanjari, The Silence of God: The Answer of the Buddha, A Dwelling Place for Wisdom, Cultural Disarmament, The Intrareligious Dialogue.*

PARANJAPE, MAKARAND, writer, translator, columnist and spiritual seeker, is Professor of English at the Jawaharlal Nehru University, New Delhi. He has been Homi Bhabha Fellow for Literature, 1991-3 and Visiting Professor, Indian Institute of Advanced Study, 1995. His books, ranging from literary criticism and poetry to anthologies and translations, include *Mysticism in Indian English Poetry; Decolonization and Development: Hind Swaraj Revisioned; The Penguin Sri Aurobindo Reader; The Best of Raja Rao* and the two latest, *Used Book* and *In Diaspora: Theories, Histories, Texts.*

RAINE, KATHLEEN, poet and scholar recognized the world over, received the CBE (Commander of the British Empire) in the New Year's Honours list of 2000. Her latest book *W. B. Yeats and the Learning of the Imagination,* captures the many facets of her rich personality including her deep understanding of the spirit of the Imagination – the central faith on which her life and work stand. She founded the Temenos Academy in 1992, of which HRH The Prince of Wales is the Patron, and to which she devotes all her energy. Among her several books are, *Selected Poems; William Blake; India Seen Afar; Autobiographies; The Human Face of God: William Blake and the Book of Job; Living with Mystery; Golgonooza: City of Imagination; Defending Ancient Springs,* and *The Presence.*

RAO, VIDYA, is a *thumri* singer par excellence and a writer on music and the performing arts. A disciple of Naina Devi, she has also trained in *khayal* with other renowned teachers. She has given recitals in India and abroad and has composed and sung for documentary films in India and for the BBC. Her work in theatre as a composer and singer has included a season at the Royal National Theatre, London. She has also received grants from the Ford Foundation and the Department of Culture, Government of India, for research on *thumri.*

REGUNATHAN, SUDHAMAHI, is Vice Chancellor, Jain Vishva Bharati University, whose interest in living folk wisdom and holistic practices in various traditions has drawn her to interact with several practitioners, leaders and renunciates belonging to several communities. She has translated papers and tracts by venerated Jain monks and published these translations in three volumes and is working on the translation of *Manan Mimamsa* by Acharya Mahaprajna. Sudhamahi has trained in Bharatanatyam dance and taught it. She has choreographed the *Panchatantra* in the idiom of dance for children. She has published a book on the faith of Arunachal Pradesh titled, *Siku: Faith and Conversion, Donyipolo Movement in Arunachal Pradesh*, and has edited a book titled, *Song of the Spirit: The World of Sacred Music*.

SAVYASAACHI is deeply involved in studying the alternative world-view of premodern cultures, and has spent several years living with the forest people of Bastar. He has worked with tribal people in Phulbani, Simlipal and other indigenous communities. He teaches sociology at Jamia Millia Islamia University, Delhi, and has published *Tribal Forest-Dwellers and Self-Rule*. He is currently working on diverse concepts of origins and on a critique of the Tiger Project in India.

SHELDRAKE, PHILIP, trained in philosophy, history and theology at the universities of Oxford and London. He is Vice-Principal of Sarum College, Salisbury, England, and Honorary Professor, University of Wales, Lampeter, and was the Hulsean Lecturer at the University of Cambridge for the year 2000. He is author of several books including *Spirituality and History*, and the more recent *Spirituality and Theology*.

SUDARSHAN, E. C. GEORGE, born in Kottayam in Kerala, is one of today's leading physicists, recognized for his work in particle theory and contribution to quantum optics. Professor Sudarshan, now Director of the Centre for Particle Theory at University of Texas, Austin, has taught in several Indian and American universities beginning with Madras Christian College, his alma mater. He has received many prestigious awards, including the C. V. Raman Award, 1970, the Padma Bhushan, 1976, and is fellow of several international learned societies and professional associations. Apart from many books on theoretical physics, he has co-authored with Tony Rothman the outstanding book, *Doubt and Certainty*, in 1998. Married to a fellow-scientist, Sudarshan does not believe in compartmentalizing scientific enquiry from the learning experience of life itself.

TANDAN, MADHU, is a writer and seeker who, along with her husband, chose to abandon a comfortable city life to join a small, self-sufficient community in the Himalaya where they spent seven years. This experience inspired her first novel, *Faith and Fire: A Way Within*. She has worked for the World Wildlife Fund, India, the Spastics Society of India and the environment group formed by the late Kamala Devi Chattopadhyay at the India International Centre. She is now working on her next book.

TYLER, PETER, is currently the Director of the Institute for Christian Spirituality at Sarum College, Salisbury. In this capacity he is especially interested in exploring new ways for Eastern and Western spiritualities to meet and dialogue. He has studied philosophy, psychology and theology at Oxford and London Universities and currently works as both lecturer and psychotherapist in the UK and abroad. He writes and lectures extensively on spirituality and his first book, *The Way of Ecstasy: Praying with Teresa of Avila*, was published in 1997. He is currently working on his next book on the relevance of the Western mystical tradition for today's world.

About the Editor

Sima Sharma has worked as a journalist and in teaching both in India and in Britain. The anthology, *Faith in an Age of Uncertainty* was compiled through her work as Editor of the *IIC Quarterly* of the India International Centre, New Delhi.

Her close friendship with Kathleen Raine drew her to the Temenos Academy of Integral Studies, London. During the ten years she lived there she was involved in issues of faith and philosophy. She worked for the International Sacred Literature Trust (ISLT) and was co-editor for the first six volumes of the ISLT series of sacred texts in translation from various world traditions.

As a seeker and thinker she is guided by the works of Sri Aurobindo and the Mother, whose influence she imbibed deeply at Pondicerry. She is married, has two daughters and lives and works in Delhi.